Experiencing
GOD'S
Compassion

August 5, 2022

Dear Carol

Delighted to share
this writing with you.
You are a 'carrier of
God's Compassion',
for others!

Thank you for your
wonderful hospitality

Love, Ginny

Experiencing GOD'S Compassion

VIRGINIA A. BLASS

Paulist Press
New York / Mahwah, NJ

Cover photo by Virginia Blass
Cover and book design by Lynn Else

Library of Congress Cataloging-in-Publication Data
Names: Blass, Virginia A., 1953– author.
Title: Experiencing God's compassion / Virginia A Blass.
Description: New York ; Mahwah, NJ : Paulist Press, [2022] | Summary: "The author weaves together fundamental aspects of our spiritual journey from personal stories, Scripture, and other spirituality writers, to invite readers to a sacred place of intimacy with God"—Provided by publisher.
Identifiers: LCCN 2021055224 (print) | LCCN 2021055225 (ebook) | ISBN 9780809155965 (paperback) | ISBN 9781587689987 (ebook)
Subjects: LCSH: God (Christianity)—Love. | Compassion—Religious aspects—Christianity. | Spirituality—Catholic Church. | Catholic Church—Doctrines.
Classification: LCC BT140 .B54 2022 (print) | LCC BT140 (ebook) | DDC 231/.6—dc23/eng/20220126
LC record available at https://lccn.loc.gov/2021055224
LC ebook record available at https://lccn.loc.gov/2021055225

ISBN 978-0-8091-5596-5 (paperback)
ISBN 978-1-58768-998-7 (e-book)

Published by Paulist Press
997 Macarthur Boulevard
Mahwah, New Jersey 07430
www.paulistpress.com

Printed and bound in the
United States of America

To my sister, Joanie
Although unable to walk or talk for her entire life,
she was my greatest teacher of compassion. My life was
profoundly blessed by her presence and love.

And to Fr. Harry Cain, SJ
My dear friend and colleague, who knew and loved Joanie,
and offered me much support and prayer throughout
this journey of accompaniment for her.

Compassion allows you to see reality;
compassion is like the lens of the heart:
it allows us to take in and understand the true
dimensions. In the Gospels, Jesus is often
moved by compassion, and compassion is
also the language of God.

Pope Francis

CONTENTS

CONTENTS

PREFACE

Over the past thirty years, while offering retreats, spiritual direction, and preached missions, I was privileged to accompany many in their spiritual journey. With great diversity of ages and circumstances in life, I listened to their common desires for the following: peace; purpose and meaning in life; ways to deal with suffering and death; and personal experience of God's love and compassion in the very reality of their lives. Most profoundly, each experienced a "breakthrough" moment in their relationship with God, leading to deeper healing, empowerment, and peace.

Reading their stories in this book, one can easily recognize that transforming moment when each person experienced God's compassion and, as a result, everything changed in his or her life. The stories also capture various dynamic aspects of our spiritual journey with God and others, identified as a "resurrection dynamic," describing our growth in faith into deeper intimacy with God, through the gift of Jesus's resurrection. Ultimately, at the heart of our spiritual journey is God's never-ending desire to draw us into a loving relationship and to invite us to be "carriers" of God's compassion for others and for our Earth-home.

We all seek to live lives full of love, happiness, and peace. God desires this for us as well. Yet, we know suffering is also a part of life. We can question, Why is there suffering when God desires our happiness and peace?

Compassion is suffering with, or as Henri Nouwen stated, "Compassion means full immersion in the condition of being human."[1] If God is full of compassion for us, have you ever considered then if God suffers with us? Many theologians, including Fr. William Barry, SJ, believed so. He said, "To come close to God is to see the world in all its reality as God sees it, and that is a painful prospect, indeed." Fr. Barry continues, "One of the reasons for such a deep-seated resistance to what we most want, closeness to God, might be that we will experience the pain of God."[2]

Enter into these personal stories and explore those aspects of our human condition through the "lens" of God's compassionate presence with us. We, too, can rediscover that God has been searching for us while we have been searching for God. Through reading these stories, Scripture, and insights, we can reclaim our own desires and continue to deepen in loving union with our compassionate God, and be "carriers" of compassion for others and for our Earth-home.

If, as a result, any reader reclaims hope and continues to seek deeper union with our loving God, in the mutual experience of compassion, the purpose of this writing will be gratefully met.

Importantly, the names and locations within these personal stories have been changed. Memories are subjective—offered from one's own point of view in an authentic way—with the hope of making a positive contribution. Questions are included at the end of each chapter for further reflection. Additional resources are also included in an appendix for further reading.

ACKNOWLEDGMENTS

My heart is full of gratitude to God and to the many who offered ongoing encouragement and support for writing this book. I worked on it during a most unprecedented year of the global pandemic outbreak of COVID-19.

I remain grateful to God for the gift of my parents and siblings, especially my sister Joanie, to whom I have dedicated this book. I am more aware than ever of how much Joanie has blessed me and taught me how to be a woman of compassion, while she remained confined to a wheelchair, unable to walk or talk. I feel her presence with me every day. My parents, Marie and Artie, gave me and all in my family a most precious gift, namely, how to be compassionate in the midst of any suffering. I feel profoundly blessed by their presence and love in my life.

I have also dedicated this book to Fr. Harry Cain, SJ, a dear friend and colleague for many years, who so compassionately accompanied me as I accompanied my parents and Joanie! His gift of humor and joy brought comfort to me in the midst of the many significant challenges associated with advocacy for a person with special needs. He knew and loved Joanie, and visited her with me whenever he was able.

Fr. Vincent Youngberg, CP (Uncle Vinny), has been one of my lifelong encouragers for many ministry invitations and experiences, as he has also been for all of my cousins! He was a renowned preacher of parish missions.

My dear friend Vicky Mishcon offered a valuable listening presence during this writing and was aware of the many challenges that arose while advocating for my sister Joanie. Her presence gave me strength.

I often checked in with my good friend Richard Alva Brown throughout this writing. His calm and optimistic attitude gave me that sense of refreshment that is so helpful. Along with his sister, Maureen Brown, I greatly appreciated their consistent support.

Mary Sheedy, PA, dear friend and colleague, has offered her time and optimism. Her suggestions related to editing and the flow of content were invaluable. I remain ever grateful to her, especially for her keen sense of humor.

Throughout this writing, I greatly appreciated all who were within my "circle of encouragement!" Many thanks to Fr. John Surette, SJ, who is a wonderful friend and a great inspiration to me. He generously shared from his writings on ecology and offered his time for our interview. I want also to express my sincere gratitude to Fr. Ken Hughes, SJ; Fr. Bill Murphy, CP; Fr. Chris Heller; Claudia Stokes; Jim and Joyce Catrombone; John Salemmo; Maureen and Rob Prohl; Karen Lewandoski; Claire Vannatta; Susie Aleksejus; Vincent Dolan; Bryan and Joyce Dolan; Georgiene Kenny;

and Br. Giancarlo Bonutti, SM. They were always available and just a phone call away.

Fr. Robin Ryan, CP, was most helpful in this publication process and offered excellent guidance. I am very grateful.

Throughout the writing of this book, I had wonderful opportunities to be introduced to others. Thank you to Sr. Mary Ann Strain, CP, director of Our Lady of Calvary Retreat Center in Farmington, Connecticut, who introduced me to her Passionist Community at Drumalis Retreat Center in Larne, Northern Ireland.

I am most grateful to my neighbor and friend, Elizabeth Lowell, for introducing me to Rev. Canon Cornelia Eaton from the Episcopal Church in Navajoland. I enjoyed interviewing Rev. Eaton very much. In addition, Fr. John Surette, SJ, generously offered his time to be interviewed for this writing, as did Tom Keevey; Fr. Steve Dunn, CP; Sr. Gail Worcelo; Sr. Margaret Rose McSparran, CP; Sr. Anna Hainey, CP; and Maura Burns, all from Drumalis Retreat and Conference Center in Larne, Northern Ireland.

I especially wish to mention my friend of many years, Fr. Bill Barry, SJ, who passed away in December 2020. Gifted in many ways, he was a prolific writer and was strict and honest with his suggestions and encouragement. I can still hear his famous comment he often offered to me with a smile: "Not bad!"

I am very grateful to those who gave permission to share from their stories in this writing. Although I changed their names and locations, I sought to honor the heart of their experience. My thanks as well to Alison Wearing for her excellent Zoom class on memoir writing (www.alisonwearing .com).

And I am so grateful for these five friends and colleagues for their generosity and support in reading and providing feedback: Fr. Harry Cain, SJ; Fr. John Surette, SJ; Fr. Robin Ryan, CP; Fr. William Murphy, CP; and Mary Sheedy, PA.

My gratitude also extends to the members of Paulist Press who assisted me, especially Diane Vescovi, senior editor, and Melene Kubat, administrative assistant and rights manager.

Chapter One

LETTING OURSELVES BE FOUND BY GOD

On my way to breakfast during a Passionist Community Chapter meeting in Jamaica, New York, several years ago, I was greeted by the late Fr. Owen Sharkey, CP, a renowned scripture scholar who was well into his senior years. I was one of several lay participants who were invited to attend this gathering.

As we walked down the long, dimly lit corridor on our way to breakfast, he addressed me: "Woman, are you walking in relationship with the real living presence of our risen Lord?"

It was 6:00 a.m. I wasn't quite awake as yet when Fr. Sharkey offered his profound question! With one eye open and the other closed, I turned and said, "Thank you, Fr. Sharkey. I promise you I will reflect more deeply upon your question, after a nice, hot cup of coffee!"

His smile lit up the darkened corridor, and as we walked, I heard his tiny chuckle. Fr. Sharkey got my attention that early morning, while the aroma of freshly brewed coffee floated up into the long hallway, beckoning us to the dining area for breakfast.

Fr. Sharkey's question impacted me and, at unpredictable moments, floated back within my awareness. We need essential questions like Fr. Sharkey's to open up that doorway into our souls. To walk in relationship with God, or with anyone, means letting ourselves be found right in the reality of our lives. When we seek God, we can come to experience that God seeks us first! It is a great grace to remind ourselves that God invites us into a loving relationship, which by its very nature is an experience of mutuality.

Our spiritual journey is like a dance between God and us. This mutual discovery begins with letting ourselves be found. It happened in the life of a man whom I shall call Francis.

THE UNLIKELY AND SURPRISING INVITATION

Whenever I preached parish missions, I always made myself available for anyone who wanted to talk about their prayer life. On this particular day Francis came to see me. He had quite a story.

Francis had raised a family, served in the military, and accumulated wealth and possessions. He lived a good life and was a devoted father and a loving husband. Now at age eighty and widowed, he had a handful of questions about God in the midst of his renewed search. He reviewed moments and experiences of his eighty years, immersed within a long-held belief that he was not in good standing with God. As our conversations continued, I listened to understand what Francis was really searching for in his relationship with God. Was it a need for forgiveness? For healing? Reconciliation? As I listened, I could tell that some of his desires were flowing from a deep-seated fear of God that he had lived with for all of his life.

"Why do I feel so distant from God? God was always like a stranger to me," Francis explained.

"Francis, you've become more aware that God seemed distant to you most of your life." I encouraged Francis to speak more about his experience of God.

"Well, Ginny, I believed that most of my life, God was really too busy for the likes of me! I didn't notice God paying attention to me. But I still went on thinking that God was somewhere, probably in that place they call 'heaven.'" Francis pointed up at the ceiling and smiled.

> *When we seek God, we can come to experience that God seeks us first!*

"It sounds like even though God seemed too busy for you in the past, you want to reconnect with God at this time in your life. You no longer want God to be a stranger," I said encouragingly.

Francis looked right at me. "Sure, as nerve-racking as that seems, that would be so different. You know, I could tell that God was close to my mom and dad."

"Francis," I invited, "what do you remember about that closeness of God with your mom and dad?"

Francis shifted in his chair to move away from the sunlight shining into his eyes. His blue eyes matched the color of his sweater. His fingers made a tapping sound on the arms of his chair, as his feet shuffled a bit underneath.

After clearing his throat, he continued his story: "I can remember as a kid, my parents took all of us to church every Sunday for Mass. There were a lot of prayers in Latin, so I had trouble paying attention. But I could tell that the Mass meant a lot to my mom and dad. For example, I could hear a light metallic clattering in the church pew, as my mom prayed her rosary. I watched her as she prayed. Her eyes were closed, and even though her mouth was moving, I couldn't hear any words. I imagined that her silent Hail Marys rose like incense carrying her long list of intercessions for all of us. I'm sure I was top on her list! When she quietly returned after receiving communion, oftentimes I noticed a tear on her cheek. Why was she crying? My dad prayed differently. He was very silent and generally kept his head down. I knew God was important for my mom and dad."

"What was that like for you, Francis, when you saw that God was important for your mom and dad?"

"I began to think that God could be closer to some people, like my mom and dad, and not others. As time went on, I just thought that I was in the second group."

"Which group would you like to be in?"

"Well, you know, it's interesting that you ask that. I was just driving past the church last week and I saw the sign announcing this parish mission. I really had no intention of coming. Sorry to say that! I've never been to a mission. But then, the sign reminded me of the missions that were offered in my church when I was a young boy. Those were the days when the church would be packed. My mom and dad went, but I stayed home."

"Did your mom and dad share about their experience of the mission with you?"

"Yes. After each evening's gathering, and when they came home, I remember how happy they seemed. Mom put her arms around me and hugged me. "I love you so much," she said with a glowing and peaceful face. As Dad passed with quickened and light steps, he roughed up my hair. I felt close to him. Soon, the aroma of roasted coffee filled the house. I figured that something good must have happened in that mission back then. So, I was kind of curious about this mission."

"I'm very happy that you are here. How's the mission going for you?"

"So far I like it. You spoke about God's compassion and unconditional love for all of us. I want that. I'm a bit on the senior side of life, so I hope it's not too late for me. That's why I wanted to speak with you. I'm trying to set things right with God. Do you think I can get God's attention?" Francis nervously asked.

He was rubbing his hands together as if warming them by a fire, and he cracked a knuckle as he waited for my response.

"Francis, it sounds like you have a very strong desire to get God's attention," I gently offered.

"Sure, I do! You invited us all to speak from our hearts to God. Well, here I am, God! Now's a good time as any, and time is running out for me."

"Consider this," I said gently. "What did you do to get your wife's attention when you had something important to say or ask?"

Francis leaned forward in his chair while he chuckled. "Oh, that's easy to answer," he immediately declared. "I would just sit down right next to her. Her name was Kathy. I'd take her hands in mine, and then I would look into her eyes. When I looked upon her beautiful, brown eyes fixed on mine, that was the time to ask my question, or say what was needed. She was right there with me," Francis said confidently.

"But how can I do that with God. He's not exactly sitting right next to me!"

"You know, Francis, prayer is really about our whole life in relationship with others and with our loving God. As you can imagine, communication is important for any relationship. Can you imagine yourself just talking with God in a similar way as you did with your wife, Kathy? Or could you imagine yourself telling God what you just told me?"

"Well, that's an interesting thought," Francis immediately replied.

"How do you feel when you consider talking to God like that?"

"Completely awkward and nervous! I'd sure like to get to that point, but maybe there's a halfway point to begin," Francis suggested.

I took time to share with Francis some additional ways to pray and listen to God. I offered suggestions in Scripture and spoke of the gift of our imaginations, and how to use both in prayer.

"I am just wondering, Francis, if you felt comfortable with any of those suggestions for your prayer today?"

Francis pondered as he stared out the window. "Well," he said. "I really appreciate hearing about all of those possibilities. Wow, this is really interesting. I think I'll start with the Scripture passage. It's like I'll have a little place to still kind of hide if I need to! That seems to be a good way to begin. I'll see how that goes. Can you pick out an easy passage for me?"

After offering a few suggestions from Scripture, we said a prayer together to end our gathering, and then Francis left. The parish mission continued. The next day, when Francis returned and entered the room, he seemed more energized. He sat down and began rubbing his hands together again. He cleared his throat as he looked intently at me.

"Welcome back, Francis. I'm delighted to be with you."

Francis leaned to his right to straighten out his left leg. "A bit of a cramp," he said. Then he fiddled with his shirt collar.

"How was your prayer with God?" I quietly asked.

"Oh yes, I uh, don't really know," Francis simply stated. "Oh yes, I did find the Scripture passage and read through it. It all sounded nice. I think I remember a priest giving a homily on that passage years ago. But nothing happened," Francis declared. "Actually, I wanted to tell you something that I realized when I tried to pray with that Scripture passage. Ginny, I'm really a stranger to the Bible! I thought it would be a good place to begin, but I felt a bit awkward reading the passage." Francis laughed nervously.

> *"I fled him down the labyrinth years of my own mind. And in the midst of tears, I hid from him."*
>
> —*Francis Thompson, "Hound of Heaven"*

"Okay. I understand. Tell me then. What have you read or experienced recently that really got your attention and touched your heart?"

With that invitation, Francis pondered. His eyes were cast down at the aged wooden floor with the uneven wide pine planks. After a long pause, he took in a deep breath and sighed deeply. Within a few moments, he looked up, snapped his fingers, and said, "I got it!" Then Francis began to recite verses from a poem with a strong and assertive voice.

"I fled him, down the days and down the nights. I fled him down arches over the years. I fled him down the labyrinth years of my own mind. And in the midst of tears, I hid from him."[1]

"Why, that's the 'Hound of Heaven' by Francis Thompson," I said.

"Yes! That's right. I loved that poem and had to memorize it as a young man. Yes, that poem captures my heart," Francis said proudly and with a smile on his face.

"Well, then, why don't you use that poem today in your prayer with God and see if that's helpful?"

"I will!" With that, Francis slowly got up out of his chair and kicked out his left leg again as if it had fallen asleep.

"I need a little oil for this ol' knee." He nodded his head toward me. "Thank you very much, I will indeed use that poem. Familiar territory!" Francis proudly stated. He whistled as he walked across the old, creaky, wooden floors, opened the door, and went on his way.

During our next visit, Francis began speaking right away. No hesitation. With a very broad smile, he said, "Hey, Ginny, you won't believe this." He took in a deep breath while he fidgeted with his eyeglasses. He ran his hands through his white hair and cleared his throat.

"That poem was wonderful! I did use it in my prayer. I found myself imagining and reviewing my life, all the while thinking that I was not in good standing with a powerful and distant God. You know, I have been afraid of God all my life."

There was a marked silence while Francis continued staring at me, as if he was waiting for my response. His body was still. His eyes locked with mine. "Yes," he said quietly. "I was afraid of God." His quiet words filled the whole room with a sense of sacredness.

"Can you say more about your fear of God?"

Francis kicked out his left leg again and this time we both heard a good crack. Then sitting up firmly in his chair, he responded, "That's a really good question. No one ever asked me that. So, it's not so easy to answer that right now. But I think it's probably related to all the years I was taught that God was keeping a record of all of my sins! I heard often of how great a sinner I was. Every Saturday I had to march over to church with my dad, no matter what the weather was like, and go to confession. If I didn't go to confession and tell all of my sins, and then I suddenly died, I would go straight to hell! No stops along the way! That's a bit scary, wouldn't you say? So, eventually as I got older, I just did not want to hear that anymore. That's when I think I stopped thinking that God listened to me. And here I am. I made it to my eighties!"

"Thank you, Francis, for sharing your story with me. I can understand your fear of God so much better. You know, Francis, a lot of times our misperceptions of God can prevent us from experiencing God's real, loving presence. And yes, here you are! You made it to your eighties. Is there anything you would like to say to God now?"

"Well, actually, yes. I really enjoyed using that poem in my prayer today. Hey, God, did I get your attention?" Francis said while turning his gaze upward and offering a broad, quizzical smile.

"Do you think you got God's attention?"

"It's funny. I think maybe God liked hearing the poem! Well, at least, I didn't hear any thunder cracks when reading it," Francis kidded. "Actually, there was more with that poem in my prayer." He straightened up in his chair.

With great ease, Francis returned to reciting the verses: "And I was defenseless utterly. I slept, and woke, I shook the hours and pulled my life upon me. I stood amid the dust of the mounded years. My days have crackled and gone up like smoke."

"Actually," he said, "there were many times that I felt as if I…shook the hours and days, and months, and years. I must have accumulated a lot of dust over the past eighty years! Imagine that."

Then looking directly into my eyes, he said, "And now, Ginny, I'm tired. I'm tired of hiding from God. I don't want to be afraid anymore. I know I'm near the end of my life, and maybe God will take that into consideration."

The sunlight illuminated his childlike expression.

"As I read this poem it was like God was still searching for me, like that hound dog image. It was as if God was really always there and still searching for me. I just didn't see. I never imagined that."

"So, Francis, you feel as if God was always there and still searching for you. And you feel so tired of being afraid of God. Francis, why do you think God is still searching for you even now?"

With that, Francis gazed downward to the old pine floor, and again pondered deeply. Raising his head slowly, with a beautiful and peaceful countenance, and with tears sliding down his face, he declared, "Why, why I think God likes me!" With that strong declaration, Francis began laughing.

"Yes, Francis, God likes you! God loves you!"

Taking out his handkerchief, Francis dabbed his watering eyes. He took in deep breaths and shook his head. "Oh gosh!" Francis said in between those breaths. "God really likes me, God loves me!" He cried gently while holding his handkerchief over his nose and mouth. Then he burst out laughing again, interrupting his own crying.

"I don't know whether to laugh or cry. This is all so new to me."

With tears still in his eyes, Francis looked at me and said, "Thank you so much. I guess I really *did* get God's attention. I think God enjoyed hearing that poem. It's a *winner*! We have some catching up to do!"

Francis spoke of his joy and amazement as he became reacquainted with his God. Now, in this tender personal experience, he discovered that God had been searching for him all his life, despite his lack of awareness. What a great gift, joy, and consolation God gave to Francis as he journeyed back through a labyrinth of the years of his life—a resurrection dynamic for Francis!

"Don't wait! Let yourselves be found by God!"

Francis came to know of a God who had great compassion for him, and not a God to fear or avoid. Francis was set free from his old, fearful images that led to his avoidance of God throughout most of his life. Who could have imagined that the verses of an old poem would later become a door leading to this great finding? Now, with his renewed, loving experience of God's personal love and compassion, Francis enjoyed God's company. I wonder what that reunion was like for God?

Francis has since gone to God. I find myself often wondering what he might say to me, or to anyone, about God. Easily, I imagine Francis kicking out his left leg, standing up proudly, and shouting out for all to hear: "Don't wait! Let yourselves be found by God!"

God desires to see our face and hear our voice. God desires our friendship. The invitation that Francis received from God is always available to us as well. Can we imagine God saying to us, "Let me see your face, let me hear your voice; for your voice is sweet, and your face is lovely" (Song 2:14).

In the next chapter, let's consider how God's compassion can empower us to forgive and deepen in peace. With forgiveness, we can participate more deeply in God's way of loving.

FOR REFLECTION

Did Francis's story resonate within your own experience in any way? Can you recall a time when you "let yourself be found by God"? What was that like for you?

Chapter Two

COMPASSIONATE OUTPOURING AND THE GRACE OF FORGIVENESS

Compassion invites forgiveness. In many situations the process of forgiveness lies at the center of our peace and happiness. Giving and receiving forgiveness is vital and necessary for our well-being and for the quality of our loving relationships.

The Dalai Lama has taught, "It is my fundamental conviction that compassion—the natural capacity of the human heart to feel concern for and connection with another being—constitutes a basic aspect of our nature shared by all human beings, as well as being the foundation for our happiness."[1] In this chapter, let's explore how the process and grace of forgiveness is deeply rooted within compassion. Indeed,

15

no relationship will mature or thrive without the ability to receive and offer forgiveness. If there was ever an aspect of our lives that exemplifies a "resurrection dynamic," it can be found in the process of forgiveness, for it can lead to healing and restoration of broken relationships.

The Gospel of Matthew says, "So when you are offering your gift at the altar, if you remember that your brother or sister has something against you, leave your gift there before the altar and go; first be reconciled to your brother or sister, and then come and offer your gift" (5:23–24). That's a powerful and direct message.

Most profoundly, we can recall the tender and compassionate story of the prodigal son (Luke 15), whose life was transformed because of his father's compassion and unconditional love. We also observe the father's vigil as he grieved the loss of his son and prayed for his return. As the story goes as follows: "So he set off and went to his father. But while he was still far off, his father saw him and was filled with compassion; he ran and put his arms around him and kissed him" (Luke 15:20). This father didn't wait for his son to arrive at his door. As he caught sight of him at a distance, he ran out to meet him.

Fr. John Donahue, SJ, offers an insightful consideration of this parable as a drama unfolding through three acts: (1) the departure of the younger son and its impact; (2) the son's return and the father's welcome; and (3) the restored relationship of the father and the older son.[2]

Understanding the law and the culture of the day, the father would have been completely free to dispose of his property during his lifetime to his sons. Therefore, this initial request by the younger son was not an unacceptable one. However, Fr. Donahue describes well the seriousness of the son's behavior, for he lost his familial, ethnic, and religious identity:[3]

> But possession of his share did not give him the rights to total disposal. He was allowed to invest the property and to use it to earn more income. He was forbidden, however, to jeopardize the capital. In a society with no benefits for the aged, the future of a parent was assured only by retention of property within the family circle. By dissipating the property, the younger son severs the bonds with his father, with his people, and hence with God; he is no longer a son of his father and no longer a son of Abraham.[4]

Soon after deciding to leave his father's home, this younger son experienced serious and painful consequences. Might we reasonably think that the son's decision to return to his father's home was greatly influenced by his experience of hunger, rather than by a desire to rejoin his family? When he remembered how his father's hired hands had plenty to eat and here he was, with the swine receiving better food than he did, he came to his senses (Luke 15:17). Reasoning that his life would be much improved by returning home, he set off. Since the son previously requested his share of inheritance when he left home, his father had every right not to welcome him back. End of story. Yet, all attention is directed toward the father's grief and his response. His silent, sorrowful vigil ended at the moment he saw his son approaching at a distance. Moved by compassion, the father rushed out, embraced him, ordered a celebratory feast, and welcomed his son back into his life! A true homecoming! His compassion was God-like and brought about a most profound restoration of relationship.

The great feast, robe, and ring were all outward signs of the restoration of a loving relationship. Upon his return, he was not relegated to be a servant, as he had expected, but was embraced as a loving son. His previous status in the family was restored, not diminished. Imagine what it must have been like for this younger son to experience the outpouring of compassion by his father.

Forgiveness is an act of compassion.

Meanwhile, let's remember the response of the older son, who never left home while he worked faithfully for his father. Learning of the feast in honor of his wayward brother, he became full of anger. Who could blame him? The older son's rather normal and predictable response is contrasted with God's ways of loving and forgiving. Human reason simply comes up short in understanding what God's compassion is like. The older son was unable to accept his father's generosity, forgiveness, and reconciliation, without looking through the lens of compassion. His anger also prevented him from entering that celebration with joy.

Forgiveness is an act of compassion. Conversely, it is our experience of compassion that enables us to go and do likewise. This father, in the likeness of Jesus, exemplified the desires of our God for us, especially for giving forgiveness.

Yet, we also know how difficult and, at times, quite impossible it is to forgive, especially when we have been severely hurt or betrayed in any way. It is at those times that we especially need God's grace. Indeed, we may simply find it impossible to enter a process of forgiveness without God's grace, for many reasons.

It helps to consider what forgiveness is not. From the writings of William Meninger, OCSO:

> Forgiveness is not forgetting. It is mindfulness. Forgiveness does not mean to condone the hurt. It is not a form of absolution, as we are not letting someone off the hook. Forgiveness is not pretense. Forgiveness is not a once-and-for-all decision. Forgiveness is not a sign of weakness, but of strength.[5]

Forgiveness requires sufficient time for understanding and for healing, and cannot be rushed. It is also important to recognize that forgiveness does not always involve or call for a physical reconciliation, especially with experiences that are more toxic or not life-giving. We can then be guided toward a more life-giving, spiritual reconciliation, by entrusting the person who caused the hurt or suffering into God's providential care. We can be empowered to move on with our lives in a deeper peace and greater interior freedom.

Let's continue to reflect upon the great grace of forgiveness as an outpouring of compassion with examples of personal stories. Perhaps you will recall an important experience of forgiveness in your life.

The late Nelson Mandela emerged from twenty-seven years in prison to become a leader in South Africa.[6] Despite all his suffering while in prison, he refused to lead with a spirit of vengeance and resentment. When asked why, he responded that otherwise he would have remained a prisoner of his past captors. He led his people with a spirit of forgiveness and compassion.[7]

PERSONAL STORY: FORGIVENESS REIGNS

My years as a special education teacher and learning disabilities specialist were challenging and rewarding. Working with students who experienced significant challenges in learning captivated my heart and was a source of great satisfaction in this new career. At the end of the day, there was always much to be very grateful for.

One particular year, my assignment involved mentoring and guiding several students who all experienced various emotional and behavioral challenges. My role was to help them achieve success within their academic classes. If any of my students engaged in disruptive behavior in the classroom, he or she would be sent to my room for me to help them process what had happened and discuss what better choices could be made in those situations. One of my students, whom I shall call Jay, was always very observant. He liked to talk. He liked to talk to me.

"Hey, Ms. B, you're off to a great start today. You're paying good attention to me!" Or I might hear Jay ask with a huge grin, "Hey, Ms. B, you need a little time out. I can see that you are getting way too busy with lots of teacher stuff! Wouldn't you rather take a break and talk with me?"

During spring break that year, I had an experience that tested my ability to forgive. This is a personal story about a deep disappointment in my relationship with Steven, whom I met some years ago during graduate studies. Back then, we had discovered how much we had in common, and we fell in love. Living a distance apart, we planned destinations that were more equidistant. This particular time, we chose Philadelphia, the "city of brotherly (and sisterly) love!"

As the weekend progressed, Steven surprisingly became more distant and aloof. During a social gathering, he spent most of his time fully engaged in conversations with others. "Well, it's important to get to know everyone, since they're your friends," he explained later to me.

As I was driving Steven back to the airport at the end of the weekend, he abruptly announced, "You know, I think we should stop seeing each other."

His words came "out of the blue," without any warning. I was not really able to see his face. "You're kidding, right?"

While cars sped by, Steven just stared ahead. "You should keep your eyes on the road while driving," he said calmly.

The late afternoon sun flickered into my eyes, as I felt tears welling up. Confused, I asked, "What about your letter that you sent me just a week ago, expressing your love?"

In a most matter-of-fact way, he replied, "Well, that was then, and this is now."

Driving about sixty-five miles an hour on a major highway in Philadelphia was not an opportune time to pull over! A heavy silence suspended our conversation. I didn't know what more to say as I felt taken completely by surprise.

Grief is a most unwelcomed visitor.

Upon arriving at the airport and driving up to the departure area for his flight, I said, "Steven, we need to talk."

"Yes, I know, but I have to catch this plane. Let's talk later." As he turned, pushed open the car door, and grabbed his suitcase, he said a quick and polite good-bye, thanked me for the weekend, and walked away to catch his plane.

I felt blindsided as I watched Steven disappear into the crowds of people rushing to make their flights. A deep sadness and hurt filled my whole being as I drove away and began the long journey home. By the fifth mile of driving in the pouring rain, my tears pushed through and dropped heavily upon my lap. I kept driving.

Brokenness happens. Relationships end. For me, a few phone calls did not resolve our separation. As time passed, the stark reality was evident—the relationship was over. My previous hopes and dreams with Steven were severed at the airport in the city of brotherly (and sisterly) love!

Grief is a most unwelcomed visitor. With its abrupt arrival, grief can pull you down into unexpected waves of painful loneliness. One day while I was teaching, I realized that my sadness was easily noticeable to others. I thought I was doing a good job of hiding my heart's brokenness. Of course, Jay, my observant student, noticed and made it a point to tell me.

"Hey, Ms. B., what's wrong with you? You're not paying as much attention to me lately. You also have a different look on your face. Hey, I know what it's like to have a really bad day, believe me. I hope you feel better," Jay said in a very kind way.

Later that evening during my prayer, my attention was drawn back to Jay's observations. Such honesty cut through my heart and brought me into a sustained silence, where the truth emerged in full, conscious awareness. God had already heard plenty of my petitions that arose from my broken heart. This deepening silence was more important than anymore words. As my gaze was drawn toward a crucifix on the wall, my heart grew still. I became aware of something or someone beyond me.

"God, help me," I prayed aloud. "I'm just here. Be with me, Jesus. Help me to be with you."

I gazed upon Jesus on the cross, pushing away darting distractions that were seeking my attention. Taking a deep breath and keeping my focus on Jesus, I felt a loving presence. Some of my heart's heaviness was lifted from my shoulders. Then, in a most peaceful and gentle way, it was as if Jesus wanted to know: "What was your reason for withholding forgiveness from Steven?"

The inner sense of Jesus's question was not condemning, but rather full of love and concern. I had plenty of reasons for withholding forgiveness and was about to present my case! Yet, while keeping my gaze upon Jesus's face as he hung on the cross, I became overwhelmed, remembering his suffering from unjust condemnation, false accusations, and ultimately crucifixion—a most horrific way to die. I recalled Jesus's prayer to his Father, while dying on the cross: "Father, forgive them; for they do not know what they are doing" (Luke 23:34).

My whole being flooded with an awareness of the importance and value of forgiveness that our triune God holds, and God's desire for all of us to receive and offer forgiveness. Even then, on the cross, forgiveness reigned! Even in the midst of our own brokenness and suffering, forgiveness reigns.

I wept. My tears washed away every excuse I previously held in defense of my lack of forgiveness. My arguments held no more power against this vulnerable, loving person of Jesus who was now tending to my broken heart in my prayer. My closed hands opened upon my lap.

After some time, I arose. I felt free. I forgave Steven. I forgave myself as a deep peace spread within me. Even when we don't intend to hurt others, brokenness happen. As devastating and painful as these experiences are, they can make or break us. Essential questions emerge. How do we proceed in the midst of this kind of brokenness? To whom do we go?

That night, I went to Jesus; or, perhaps, Jesus came to me in a most quiet and tender way. As a result, I became freer to forgive. It was all grace from God.

Pope Francis speaks often about the grace of gazing upon the face of Jesus. "He always looks at us with love. He asks us something, he forgives us, and he gives us a mission," Pope Francis said during one of his early morning Masses in the Domus Sanctae Marthae. That was true for me.

Then I remembered that my parish was celebrating the sacrament of reconciliation that night. We can erroneously think that forgiveness is just a personal experience that does not affect others and so remain blind to the communal dimension of forgiveness. The way we love others is the way we love God, and the way we love God is the way we love others.

The priest-confessor listened attentively to my experience. "My friend, you have received a great grace from God. You have experienced all three dimensions of forgiveness, namely: forgiveness, healing, and reconciliation."

This reconciliation for me, though, was more spiritual and not physical, because I realized that it would not have been life-giving to return to that relationship with Steven. Before leaving, I prayed for any healing and peace for Steven, too. And as I left the deeply quiet place of worship, I softly said, "Brokenness happens. Forgiveness reigns!"

Back in my classroom the next day, sure enough, Jay approached me. If I ever needed a significant sign of my own healing, Jay would be the one to offer it. "Hey, Ms. B., I've been noticing something different with you. Looks like you're having a better day today. You know what? I think you're finally back to your old self. You're paying more attention to me," Jay happily declared!

> *We need God's abundant and available grace, especially for forgiveness.*

Something changed deep within me in that whole prayer experience. What I was unable to do on my own, I carried out with the grace of God. I also took the opportunity to speak with Steven by phone one night. It was a very brief conversation, but brought about more understanding, a sense of closure, and peace for both of us. That was good. God is good.

We need God's abundant and available grace, especially for forgiveness. Since then, I have collected some insightful quotes about forgiveness, and offer them to close this chapter.

N. T. Wright wrote in *Evil and the Justice of God,*

When we forgive someone, we not only release them from the burden of our anger and its possible consequences; we release ourselves from the burden of whatever it was they had done to us, and form the crippled emotional state in which we shall go on living if we do not forgive them and instead cling to our anger and bitterness.[8]

Peter Van Breeman, SJ, said, "Resentment is an acid which consumes its container. Forgiveness is the completion of love. People who do not forgive remain in the power of those who injured them."[9]

More than that, a Chinese proverb says, "The person who does not learn how to forgive must learn to dig two graves!"

Lastly, from Archbishop Desmond Tutu:

I told [those serving on the Truth and Reconciliation Commission] that the cycle of reprisal and counter reprisal that had characterized their national history had to be broken and that the only way to do this was to go beyond retributive justice to restorative justice, to move on to forgiveness, because without it there was no future.[10]

We considered how personal experience of Jesus's compassion not only heals us but can empower us to offer and receive forgiveness, especially when we are unable to do so on our own. There are also times in our lives when we can experience a certain "powerlessness" and then errone-ously believe we are moving away from God. Yet, another profound invitation from God may be happening that can remain unnoticed if we are not paying attention. We will consider this in the following chapter.

FOR REFLECTION

Can you recall a personal story of forgiveness in your life that was significant? What are you most grateful for in relation to that experience?

Chapter Three

THE RESURRECTION OF OUR POWERLESSNESS

> But he said to me, "My grace is sufficient for
> you, for power is made perfect in weakness."
> So, I will boast all the more gladly of my
> weaknesses, so that the power of Christ may
> dwell in me. Therefore I am content with
> weaknesses, insults, hardships, persecutions,
> and calamities for the sake of Christ; for
> whenever I am weak, then I am strong.
>
> 2 Corinthians 12:9-10

The great gift and grace of forgiveness, as we considered in the previous chapter, can lead us into healing and trans-formation. We also recognize that this process at times can be very difficult and may also lead to experiences of powerlessness in our journey with God and others. We can misperceive any experiences of powerlessness, and erroneously believe that we are losing faith or disappointing God and others. Let's consider through Scripture and personal stories how some experiences of powerlessness can be invitations from God to deepen in intimacy.

The invitation in 2 Corinthians 12:9–10 (above) is perhaps one of the most challenging to understand and difficult to accept. We could question whether our normal hopes and desires for achievement, success, promotions, and financial security go against this invitation. Yet, couldn't we also wonder why anyone would choose to live a life more defined by weakness and powerlessness than by success and financial abundance? This is at the heart of Christian paradox!

The Scripture story of Mary Magdalene in the Gospel of John, chapter 20, offers much encouragement for this consideration of Christian paradox and experiences of powerlessness. Here we read about the tender encounter between Mary and Jesus, as risen Lord, at a time when Mary experienced tremendous grief, confusion, and powerlessness. In mutual searching and discovery, Mary deepened in her faith and love with her risen Lord, even in the midst of her grief and sorrow. Just as with Mary, the sorrow of our lives can become, by grace, a passageway to deeper intimacy with Jesus, and lead us into a "resurrection dynamic."[1]

A lot of ink has been spilled over the years about the life of Mary Magdalene. Despite several erroneous portrayals of her life, she was a very well-respected woman in early Christianity. Much of her life remains unknown. Was she married? Did she have any children? Because the title of her name does not identify any relationship with a man, namely, wife of, or daughter of, scripture scholars suggest that Mary Magdalene was not married. What they seem to agree upon is that Mary Magdalene left the security of her home in Magdala after she encountered Jesus and, as a result, received a significant healing.

Luke 8:1–3 says, "Soon afterwards he went on through cities and villages, proclaiming and bringing the good news of the kingdom of God. The twelve were with him, as well as some women who had been cured of evil spirits and infirmities: Mary, called Magdalene, from whom seven demons had gone out, and Joanna, the wife of Herod's steward Chuza, and Susanna, and many others, who provided for them out of their resources."

The nature of Mary Magdalene's healing remains unknown to this day. Was her healing more physical or emotional? However, as a result of her encounter with Jesus, she experienced a tremendous conversion and healing, and then left her home and life to follow and serve him in his ministry.

Scripture reveals as well that Mary Magdalene was one of the women along with Mary, the mother of Jesus, who were present during his passion and death on the cross. Mary witnessed the horrific and tragic manner of Jesus's death. Imagine her grief, her loss, her confusion. Yet, in the midst of such great powerlessness, Mary emerges later with a new hope and a new identity, and is commissioned by Jesus as the first "Apostle to the Apostles," a title attributed to her by St. Augustine. Her new song was transformed from one of dark grief to joy as she declared, "I have seen the Lord!" (John 20:18).

What possibly could have transpired in this encounter with her risen Lord to bring about such radical transformation out of the depths of her great powerlessness? How could her intense sorrow be changed into joy?

> "They have taken away my Lord, and I do not know where they have laid him."
>
> —John 20:13

A part of that answer surely involves the reality and dynamics of a faith-filled relationship. In John's Gospel, we read of Mary's journey to the tomb in the early morning to complete the burial process for the body of Jesus. The descriptive words "while it was still dark" (John 20:1) suggest that Mary was progressing in her faith in Jesus, for she at first misinterpreted the significance of the empty tomb. Perhaps she was still blinded by her own emotional experience of "uninformed" grief. She may have believed that Jesus's body was stolen, as she observed that "the stone had been removed from the tomb" (v. 1). How devastating. Filled with great sorrow and confusion, perhaps she pondered what would become of her, the disciples, and the mission of Jesus.

She ran to find Peter. "They have taken the Lord out of the tomb, and we do not know where they have laid him" (v. 2). Both Peter and another disciple ran to the tomb and discovered it empty, as Mary had described. It is reasonable to think that they, too, felt overwhelmed, frightened, and confused. What else could they do but return home? Mary did not:

> Mary stood weeping outside the tomb. As she wept, she bent over to look into the tomb; and she saw two angels in white, sitting where the body of Jesus had been lying, one at the head and the other at the feet. They said to her, "Woman, why are you weeping?" She said to them, "They have taken away my Lord, and I do not know where they have laid him." When she had said this, she turned around and saw Jesus standing there, but she did not know that it was Jesus. Jesus said to her, "Woman, why are you weeping? For whom are you looking?" Supposing him to be the gardener, she said to him, "Sir, if you have carried him away, tell me where you have laid him, and I will take him away." Jesus said to her, "Mary!" She turned and said to him in Hebrew, "Rabbouni!" (which means Teacher). Jesus said to her, "Do not hold on to me, because I have not yet ascended to the Father. But go to my brothers and say to them, 'I am ascending to my Father and your Father, to my God and your God.'" (John 20:11–17)

At first, Mary did not recognize that the stranger was Jesus. But then, within a most tender moment, Mary knew. Mary recognized Jesus's voice when he called her by her name, "Mary." Mary's change in salutation from "Sir" to

"Rabbouni" may suggest a maturation in her relationship with Jesus, from a stranger to a teacher.

Mary needed to progress through a threshold, through an "unresurrected powerlessness."[2] Mary had to first stand in the truth of her own powerlessness, as she let go of the previous ways of recognizing Jesus. Nothing in her mind, intelligence, or reasoning could explain these events, or her present experience in the garden. Something new was emerging in her relationship with Jesus as gift and grace from Jesus's resurrected life, namely the call to deepen in faith.

The risen Jesus called forth a more mature faith in this new way of being in relationship with him. The old way of knowing by "sight" was no longer effective. Isn't it true that we have special names or nicknames for those we love? Likewise, isn't it true that we recognize the voice of someone who loves us?

Can we imagine that Mary proceeded through an "unresurrected powerlessness" into a "resurrected powerlessness" in her faith journey?[3] That resurrection happens when we, in the midst of our powerlessness, freely choose to act in a trusting way, even when we cannot fully understand what is happening. Who can explain this? This is at the heart of our Christian paradox in which the virtues of faith, hope, and charity become ways for our empowerment. As a result of her encounter, and Mary's newly deepened faith, she received a special commission from Jesus, as she was sent back into her life to become Apostle to the Apostles. She declared, "I have seen the Lord!" (John 20:18). Jesus's commissioning was also a sign of Mary's continued maturation in her faith relationship.

Mary's journey from powerlessness into deeper faith is similar to ours. The victory over darkness has been won through the passion and death of Jesus, and his gift of resurrected life. For a resurrection to happen within us, we too have to let go of whatever inhibits our faith development and die to self in any aspect that impedes our growth in faith. We too can become empowered to mature in our faith relationship with Jesus, especially by choosing to act with greater faith, hope, and charity. In so doing, we, like Mary Magdalene, deepen in our relationship with Jesus.

Fr. William Barry, SJ, has written much about God's desires for a mutual, loving relationship with us, a friendship. God never stops searching for us or inviting us into loving friendship. "If God invites us into the community life of the Trinity, then God desires a relationship of mutuality with us."[4] The following personal story illustrates giving witness to our growth in faith through an experience of unresurrected powerlessness.

TWO LETTERS

"Everyone has to die someday, and no one can do it for you," my mom once said to me, while we sat outside on a warm springlike afternoon at the nursing home. Undeniable truth. But when death unexpectedly arrives for someone young, is our grief more unbearable?

I have listened to many people painfully express profound sorrow at the tragic loss of their loved one. The shock, the injustice, the stark emptiness, tears at the very center of our being, rendering us, at least for a time, in a spiraling darkness of grief. Powerless. Even there and even then, there is light. We just are unable to see it, for we are blinded and overwhelmed by our grief. Normal routines and expectations have been shattered while we search for peace and healing.

"The joy of our hearts has ceased; our dancing has been turned to mourning" (Lam 5:15).

After returning from a wonderful visit with friends who were living in England, I began packing a suitcase again and was going to drive up to see Jack, who was staying with a mutual friend. But in the meantime, I had something very important to talk to Jack about that I came to realize when I was away.

I called the home of our friend Roy and said excitedly, "I'm looking so forward to visiting with you all tomorrow. Can you please put Jack on the phone?" There was no response.

"Roy, is Jack there? I'd love to just say a quick hello to him." Roy was silent.

Then, without warning, and with a steady and serious speaking voice, Roy replied, "Ginny, I have to tell you something. While you were away, Jack was in a terrible car accident. He's already dead and buried. I'm so sorry. I couldn't reach you when you were out of the country." He said this so directly, but his shaky voice stuttered while delivering this shocking message. There was no good time to tell me.

"I'm so sorry," Roy kept repeating. His stark words became like a knife cutting through my heart. Gasping, I felt faint.

"Roy, I need to sit down." I couldn't take in any more conversation. "Sorry Roy, I need to go for now." Feeling weak, I hung up the phone and sat down on the nearest chair.

This unexpected announcement dissolved and disrupted the peaceful silence of just five minutes before. Noises from the apartment below me seemed to echo off the walls of my apartment, where I sat motionless. I felt cut off from the land of the living as a noticeable numbness spread within my muscles. I had no energy. My breathing was labored as my heart weighed heavily within me. I held my face and wept, all alone in my apartment. Jack's dead.

Such announcements break into our awareness in painful segments. The initial shock tears open our heart and dissolves all of our expectations of what was supposed to happen in any given day. The stark reality that we can no longer gaze upon the face of our loved one, or hear their voice, or feel their embrace, slowly pours into reality. We think surely death will not come to my dear one, so young. That's how we live our lives. That's how I was living my life, but everything changed with that phone call.

I loved Jack and had hoped we would share our lives together. A pervasive sense of loss and separation folded in upon me like an approaching fog. While trying to stay busy to counterbalance this intense grief, my concentration was bombarded with the repetition of Roy's words and message:

"Ginny...while you were away, Jack was killed in a terrible car accident." Shock embraced my entire being.

My anticipated day's plans dissolved as tears now fell upon my lap. The early morning sun shone on the empty chairs in my apartment. No appetite. No conversations. My heart ached with every beat. Anguish threw its heavy nets over my constricted heart and grief-stricken body. At times I couldn't move.

Like Mary Magdalene, I found no body.

I cried out, "Jack, I didn't get to see you! I didn't get to talk with you! I can't believe you are dead!"

"Because of this our hearts are sick, because of these things our eyes have grown dim" (Lam 5:17).

I moved through the hours of the next few days by establishing a short list of things to do. I used every bit of concentration to accomplish something on the list, no matter how small or insignificant. I made my bed. I ate breakfast. If I could, I made a phone call to a friend. The rhythm of time radically changed and poured forth unannounced waves of grief. Life appeared to go on as usual for all around me, while I labored to get through the next hour.

Since I was out of the country when Jack died—unable to attend his wake or funeral—I did not immediately believe that Jack was dead. Like Mary Magdalene, I found no body. With the passing days, weeks, and months, that unwanted visitor, grief, continued to carve out an empty space deep within my heart. It became a place of diminished light, where hope was also fading. A gripping sense of powerlessness filled my whole being. Have you been there?

Then, light began to break through in unexpected ways when I was invited to go away on a retreat of length. Having no excuse and standing in great need, I graciously accepted without knowing what to expect on those eight days in silence and prayer.

As the retreat unfolded, I spoke of my recent experience of loss with my spiritual director, Sr. Peg. She invited me to do something rather simple, yet profound: "Go and write a letter to Jack and tell him what you never were able to tell him."

When I left her office, I went outside with a notebook in hand, and began writing:

Jack, everything has changed, as I have to learn how to live without you. Can I? I don't want to. When I'm in a crowd, I sometimes think I see you when a person looks just like you. I don't stare, though. I can still remember the sound of your voice. I don't believe you're dead, Jack. The worst part of my day is when I first wake up, as dread from this unchangeable separation drains my energy and the inner struggle begins all over again. You know, I had a strong sense of your cologne when I was on that flight to England, as if you were sitting right next to me in the empty seat. I later learned that it was near the exact moment of your death. Oh, God, I miss you, Jack.

Tears were streaming down my checks as I finished writing my letter to Jack. I felt a sense of completeness in giving voice to what was unspoken. "Hey, God, can you please make sure that Jack receives this letter," I said while gazing upward. "Express mail!"

Then, in a moment of inspiration, I began writing a second letter, only this time, it was from Jack to me! "Why not, I pondered?" This one was easier, for some reason, and I completed it rather quickly. While reading this second letter aloud on that very hot, humid day outside, where the air was completely still, I felt a gentle, fragrant breeze touch my cheek, like a kiss! The heaviness that had occupied my heart for so long was released, and the knife lodged there for so long…was gone.

In that moment, I believed that Jack loved me, too. Tears streamed from my eyes and a deep peace filled my whole being. It was as if I walked out of that tomb of my own grief into the light of a new day. "Thank you, God, so much. Thank you, Jack. I love you, too."

As my retreat continued, Sr. Peg invited me to pray using the Scripture story of Mary Magdalene at the tomb of Jesus. I began to wonder if maybe I, too, had to pass through a threshold of faith, similar to Mary Magdalene's experience, and stand inside the truth of my loss and grief. There was nothing I could do to change the reality or the impact on my life from the sudden and tragic death of the person I loved.

I, too, had to let go of the previous way of knowing and loving Jack and of the future I had hoped to enjoy with him. I needed to embrace this painful powerlessness that was for so long unresurrected and hold my sorrow in full and painful awareness before God. I surrendered into this truth.

Most profoundly, during my prayer, I felt as if Jesus tended again to my broken heart. I was no longer alone in this grief—my loss seemed to matter to him. Jesus's personal offering of compassion for me was the most profound source of my healing.

> We *are people of the* resurrection, *not tomb dwellers*!

In that healing, I took comfort in my belief that Jack is present with God, and within the communion of all who have died before him. Even though I was taught that for years, I now truly believed it. With that freshly embraced conviction, a tiny light of hope returned.

Hope can be restored as we experience Jesus's personal love and compassion for us. Our loss, our suffering matters to God. Death now no longer has the same power over me as it did before. "Where, O Death, is your victory? Where, O Death, is your sting?" (1 Cor 15:55).

Everything on the Earth and in the whole cosmos has been transformed by God's desire, and the gift of Jesus's resurrection. We are people of the *resurrection*, not tomb dwellers! Without receiving this grace of resurrection dynamic, we can remain vulnerable to constructing egocentric views about life and death. We can be absorbed by the present-day culture with all of its lures and empty promises, and can then live as if we will go on forever, or live as if there is nothing more to life than what meets the eye. Our hope can diminish as we lose awareness of our very call and God's dream for us and all Creation to live in the likeness of Jesus, in peace, justice, and compassion for all.

Richard Rohr, OFM, offers the following about an experience of resurrection:

> The "cross," rightly understood, always reveals various kinds of resurrection. It's as if God were holding up the crucifixion as a cosmic object lesson, saying: "I know this is what you're experiencing. Don't run from it. Learn from it, as I did. Hang there for a while, as I did. It will be your teacher. Rather than losing life, you will be gaining a larger life. It is the way through." As impossible as that might feel right now, I absolutely believe that it's true.[5]

On those days of retreat with Sr. Peg, I learned that the smallest amount of light casts out any amount of darkness. The light remains. No darkness can put out the light within, the Christ Light! Jesus teaches us how to recognize his voice even in profound darkness or desolation.

The paradoxes of our life might, at first, take us by surprise and knock us off our feet. There is a pathway through the darkness, which each one of us can discover, that leads toward the light. This light can arrive in the gentlest ways: an invitation from a friend, speaking with a person who knows and loves us, or our prayer with God. Hope enables us to stand in the reality of our loss or suffering and still see a glimpse of light for our future. We then can discover that we are stronger and more compassionate than before.

John O'Donohue describes darkness as one of our closest companions: "It can never really surprise us; something within us knows the darkness more deeply than it knows the light. In the beginning was the darkness. The first light was born out of the dark."[6]

In the next chapter, we will explore this grace of compassion as an "incurable wound" of mutuality with God.

FOR REFLECTION

Can you recall a time when you experienced an "unresurrected powerlessness"? What was that like for you? What did you do?

Chapter Four

GOD'S COMPASSION— LIKE AN *INCURABLE WOUND* FOR US

Meister Eckhart (1260–1327), Dominican theologian and mystic, said that "the very first outpouring of God is compassion." Compassion means to "suffer with."

What is your image of God? Do you still have the same image of God as from your childhood? Do you remember how you came to form your image of God? Was it from what others taught you? What about your personal experience of God? Have your personal experiences changed your image of God in any way?

I have listened to many speak of their experiences of God in prayer, and how they carried images of God that seemed to be more a projection of their earlier parental experiences. When a person had experiences of a very demanding and strict father, oftentimes God was imaged in a similar way. When one's father was very kind and loving, it was so easy for that person to imagine God as loving. Many have imaged God as Mother as their relationship with God grew and matured.

The image of God that we carry within, for various reasons, directly impacts how we relate to God. I often say, "Let your direct experience of God inform and form your image." In other words, any experiences of avoiding God or being afraid to get close to God may be more the result of our projecting false images onto God. We can also hold onto uncharacteristic images of God concerning suffering.

> I *believed* *God* *was* *somehow* *protected* *from* *ever* *experiencing* *suffering.*

We may carry an image of God who is unaffected by our suffering. We may think that somehow God is above that kind of experience or protected from suffering. Yet, Jesus certainly, as the person of God who fully experienced being human, suffered immensely in his passion and death. We can recall in John 11:35 that "Jesus wept" (NABRE). Each Lent, we ask for the grace to know Jesus more intimately, so that we can love him and follow him more intimately. Jesus suffered.

Have you ever considered if God suffers with us? Is God affected by our sufferings and plights? Does God want us to know about his sorrow? Is this a place of mutuality with our

God? Reflections upon those essential questions may help us to become more aware of our desires for closeness with God, and of the depth of compassion that God has for us and all of Creation. Can our experience of suffering bring us closer to God and others? If you came to believe that God is affected by our suffering and that God suffers with us, would God become more vulnerable and approachable? These questions are at the heart of the sharing in this chapter.

In my earlier years, I had an image of a very loving God, who was a powerful and omnificent Creator of all life, fully aware of our sufferings and sins but *not affected* by our suffering. I believed God was somehow protected from ever experiencing suffering, but that image has changed over the years.

That previous image no longer describes the God whom I have come to experience, or as others have experienced and shared with me. I have met God who is present with me in my suffering, and as a result, my life and my relationship with God changed. Over the years, I have come to associate the descriptive words *incurable wound*[1] with God's sorrow, especially after reading the story of the prophet Jeremiah in chapter 30. In addition to Jeremiah, scripture scholars of both the New and Old Testaments have expressed their strong belief in a God who suffers with us.

As noted earlier, Fr. William Barry, SJ, has reflected much upon God's suffering in his article, "God's Sorrow":

> To come close to God is to see the world in all its reality as God sees it, and that is a painful prospect indeed. One of the reasons for such a deep-seated

resistance to what we most want, closeness to God, might be that we will experience the pain of God.[2]

Additionally, Fr. Richard Rohr, OFM, offers this consideration of the suffering of God: "I believe—if I am to believe Jesus—that God is suffering love. If we are created in God's image and if there is so much suffering in the world, then God must also be suffering. How else can we understand the revelation of the cross?"[3]

Catholic scripture scholar Fr. Robin Ryan, CP, teaches, "We cannot know what Divine suffering is like. God is affected, yet remains God. This divine compassionate solidarity with human suffering manifests the depths of God's love."[4]

Certain poets and mystics have described their intimate experience of God's love as a wound. Thirteenth-century mystic poet Jalaluddin Rumi wrote,

You try to be faithful
And sometimes you're cruel.
You are mine. Then, you leave.
Without you, I can't cope.

And when you take the lead,
I become your footstep.
Your absence leaves a void.
Without you, I can't cope.

You have disturbed my sleep,
you have wrecked my image.

You have set me apart.
Without you, I can't cope.[5]

We also find this language in the writings of St. John of the Cross (1542–91), a Spanish Catholic priest and most notable mystic. He wrote from the depths of his own profound experiences of God. In *The Dark Night of the Soul*, he poetically describes a most intimate, loving experience of God as a "wound of love":

O guiding night!
O night more lovely than the dawn!
O night that has united
the Lover with his beloved,
transforming the beloved in his Lover....

When the breeze blew from the turret,
as I parted his hair,
it wounded my neck
with its gentle hand,
suspending all my senses.

I abandoned and forgot myself,
laying my face on my Beloved;
all things ceased; I went out from myself,
leaving my cares
forgotten among the lilies.[6]

The writings of St. John of the Cross are challenging to understand, yet offer a sense of his intimate relationship with

God. St. John clearly chose the verb "wounded" to describe his experience.

The image of wound is presented in Jeremiah 30. Through the prophet Jeremiah, God revealed that the people of Judah were suffering from a wound that will not heal of itself, and that Yahweh intervened and restored his people. The wound described Israel's corruption and God's attempt, through his prophet Jeremiah, to persuade the people to reform and turn back to God. At the time when his people were exiled in Babylon, Jeremiah encouraged the exiles that their suffering would come to an end and their relationship with Yahweh would be restored. As a faithful prophet, Jeremiah spoke intimately of his suffering and the suffering of his people:

> Then the LORD put out his hand and touched my
> mouth; and the LORD said to me,
> "Now I have put my words in your mouth!"
>   (Jer 1:9)

> My joy is gone, grief is upon me,
>   my heart is sick.
> Hark, the cry of my poor people
>   from far and wide in the land:
> "Is the LORD not in Zion?
>   Is her King not in her?"
> ("Why have they provoked me to anger with
>   their images,
>   with their foreign idols?")

"The harvest is past, the summer is ended,
  and we are not saved."
For the hurt of my poor people I am hurt,
  I mourn, and dismay has taken hold of me. (Jer
  8:18–21)

Jeremiah desired that his people would see how God had entered into the anguish of their situation and made it his very own. In so doing, Jeremiah witnessed to the compassion of God in their midst. As their prophet, Jeremiah knew the suffering of the people of God and came to know the anguish of God who suffered with his people in having an incurable wound. Compassion is at the heart of Jeremiah's experience with God and his people.

Scripture scholar Terence Fretheim identified that the prophet Jeremiah "embodies the suffering of God."[7] Fretheim explains that "the prophet had a relationship with God that no other individual enjoyed; it was of such a character that the prophet's life was increasingly reflective of the divine life. This relationship means that no separation can be made between the suffering of the prophet and the suffering of God."[8]

God's desire for intimacy with the people of Israel is expressed in Jeremiah 3:19–22:

I thought
  how I would set you among my children,
and give you a pleasant land,
  the most beautiful heritage of all the nations.

And I thought you would call me, My Father,
    and would not turn from following me.
Instead, as a faithless wife leaves her husband,
    so you have been faithless to me, O house of
        Israel,
                       says the LORD.

A voice on the bare heights is heard,
    the plaintive weeping of Israel's children,
because they have perverted their way,
    they have forgotten the LORD their God:
Return, O faithless children,
    I will heal your faithlessness.

Here we come to you;
    for you are the LORD our God.

Fretheim expresses God's disappointment in this way: "God is like a person who has been rejected not only by his spouse but by his children as well. God suffers the effects of the broken relationship at multiple levels of intimacy. The wounds of God are manifold."[9] And "God is revealed not as one who remains coolly unaffected by the rejection of the people, but as one who is deeply wounded by the broken relationship."[10] Fretheim continues to present a hopeful outcome because of God's compassion. "In spite of the suffering God undergoes, God's salvific will does not waver; God's steadfast love endures forever. In this respect, God offers the supreme example of what to do with suffering."[11]

> *God is with us in our own suffering and is*
> *affected by our suffering.*

Old Testament scripture scholar Rabbi Abraham Heschel has written of God's pathos. The word *pathos* comes from the Greek word meaning "suffering" and implies that one is suffering because of love. "He (God) is moved and affected by what happens in the world, and reacts accordingly."[12] Rabbi Heschel believed that the prophet is someone whose emotions are in harmony with God's. "To be a prophet," says Heschel, "means to identify one's concern with the concern of God."[13]

Rabbi Heschel also believed that we are called to do God's work by becoming more conscious of our sharing in his (God's) pathos. "God is the most moved mover; a God of great pathos, who weeps when people suffer, is angered when they mistreat one another and gladdened when they pursue the right and the good. Prophecy consists in the inspired communications of divine attitudes to the prophetic consciousness."[14] God is with us in our own suffering and is affected by our suffering.

For Rabbi Abraham Heschel, God's pathos means that God is never neutral or uninvolved with the world's events. Indeed, Rabbi Heschel believed that God is involved and affected by issues of injustice or oppression in its many forms. "The prophets never identify God's pathos with His essence, because for them the pathos is not something absolute, but a form of relation."[15]

In the Book of Job, we find a story in Scripture that seeks answers to why a good person suffers. Fr. Robin Ryan, CP, explains that in Job, God is presented as one who suffers with him. After Job's lengthy dialogue with God, Job did not receive an answer from God about the "why" of suffering. He did, however, receive an intimate experience of God's loving presence in the midst of his suffering, which was at the heart of his transforming experience. Fr. Ryan teaches that God can be trusted even in the darkness of human suffering because God hears our lament and responds. Chaos does not reign, as Fr. Ryan teaches, but God's compassion does. Truly, our God desires to be present with us in all things, especially in our suffering. Just as with Job's experience, our suffering may not be removed, but we can carry our suffering differently when we know and experience God's compassionate presence with us.[16]

Previously I shared an experience of personal loss and grief. My healing from God was not through the removal of the suffering or changing aspects of the situation, but through my personal experience of God's compassion. Remarkably, I felt God weeping with me, too. Like Job, God's compassion for me was the deepest source of my own inner healing and a resurrection dynamic that led me into deeper peace.

In some mysterious but real way, God's compassion for us means that God is affected by our suffering. Compassion is a place of mutual intimacy with our God, where we can be ourselves in the loving presence of God. Additionally, we are invited to participate in God's desires and legacy by becoming carriers of God's incurable wound for others. We become in the likeness of those we love. Let's consider this more in the next chapter.

FOR REFLECTION

Recall a time in your life when you experienced God's compassion, or pathos, for you? What was that like for you? What was God like to you?

Chapter Five

BEING CARRIERS OF GOD'S COMPASSION FOR OTHERS

From this experience of Christ's healing presence in our lives, each of us is commissioned to embody the compassion of Christ in the world.

Robin Ryan, CP[1]

Being "carriers of God's compassion" for others brings us into deeper intimacy with God, as we experience being sent by God to help others. Where has God sent you? Oftentimes, our commissioning can lead us to other countries to help those in need. We think of missionaries. Perhaps we imagine that since we are not missionaries sent out to help others, we may not be carriers of God's compassion for others. Not true! A very special place of "sending" happens right in our homes, and with our families and friends. That was true for me. Here is a personal story about my sister, Joanie, that gives an example of being sent right in the present reality of our lives.

"Can Joanie come home with us?" I asked just before my mother and father were about to head directly toward that towering, haunted-looking building.

"Stay in the car. We'll be right back," my father replied, as he and Mom walked quickly on the long, gravel driveway. I knew they were going to pick up Joanie, my older sister, after a two-week respite time for my mom. I didn't understand what this place was about, but the two weeks were up.

My siblings were content with reading a book, while I preferred leaning out the window, watching my parents go inside the huge building. My hand only reached about halfway down the side of the car door, so I couldn't reach the tall grass below.

"I think it's going to rain," I said aloud. I could smell that distinctive ozone in the air, and the tiny leaves on the tress were overturning. The clouds above were darkening while the birds sat so quietly on tree limbs. A baby rabbit hopped near the car, busy eating the freshly cut grass. "If it wasn't for this rabbit, I'd be bored," I thought. I wondered if the rabbit enjoyed the aroma of the sweet grass as much as I did. "Hey, Mister Rabbit, do you know that it is going to rain soon?" He continued to wiggle his nose and enjoy the meal of sweet grass.

"What's taking them so long?" I asked, turning my face back inside the car so my siblings could hear. The rabbit darted briskly away into the woods because a rhythmical gravel sound was becoming louder and louder. I looked up to see my parents walking toward us. "Where is Joanie?" I questioned.

My father had his arm around my mother's shoulder and her head was lowered. As they approached, I noticed how pale Mom looked even though she had some makeup on. She raised a tissue to her face and held it there. Dad opened the passenger front door and she slowly slipped in. Before Dad got in on the driver side, Mom turned slowly, looking over her shoulder, and said, "What are we going to do?" When I saw her watery eyes, my stomach began to tighten. "This doesn't sound good," I thought to myself.

That was the first time my older brother looked so worried. That was the first time I ever heard my mother express any worry about Joanie. That was the first time I saw tears in Mom's eyes. I felt nervous as my father started the engine and slowly turned the car around in the driveway. We were heading home.

"Where's Joanie?" I cautiously asked.

My father quietly responded, "She's not ready yet to come home."

> *That was the first time I ever heard my*
> *mother express any worry about Joanie.*

About a week later, they went back to that institution to pick up Joanie and take her home. My mom cried because

Joanie looked pale and very tired, and she did not act like her usual self. Joanie's eyes were dilated. Something was wrong.

"I think they sedated her to keep her quiet," I overheard Dad say.

Mom stared in shock at my father and then at Joanie in disbelief, and wiped away her tears. "Will she be okay?" Mom said sadly, continuing to stroke Joanie's face and observe her with the sustained gaze of a mother's love.

That's all I would ever hear my parents say about that stay for Joanie, as they did not want to cause any worry for the rest of us. I did not need their explanations, though. Mom's pale and tightened face fought to hold back an outpouring of anguished tears. As her face disappeared behind the tissue, I silently questioned, "What happened to Joanie?"

That time away was supposed to be a good experience for Joanie and one in which my mom could receive some much-needed respite. The well-intentioned decision did not turn out the way my parents desired. We will never know what really happened to Joanie because she was completely unable to tell us. That facility for the developmentally disabled has long since been shut down by the state because of continual complaints.

That was when I came to realize the serious situation of my sister's life and the need for her constant care. I was too young to explain what I was feeling, but my heart was with Joanie forever. Every day, I watched my parents care for her and I helped wherever I could. I began to pay close attention to Joanie.

Joanie was born very prematurely, weighing about one and a half pounds at birth and needing intensive care. During that whole process, apparently, she did not receive adequate amounts of oxygen and suffered brain damage. Back then, little was known about how to care for premature babies. When she was able to be taken home from the hospital, the doctors told my parents their baby would not live past the age of four. They later learned that she had cerebral palsy and would never walk or talk.[2]

My parents probably expected that Joanie would die in her childhood years as the doctors had predicted. I also imagine that they kept doing everything they could for her, while bracing themselves for that inevitable day. Those early predictions, however, never came true.

One of the best ways to care for and get to know someone who cannot walk or talk is to observe them and identify patterns of behavior. What events or circumstances seemed to make Joanie feel happy? Was there any pattern to understand when she cried or was in pain? I had an ever-growing curiosity and desire to understand Joanie better.

"Mom, does Joanie eat everything? Does she like vegetables?"

"Yes, just about everything. She has a great appetite," she replied with a smile.

"How do you know when she's had enough?"

"Well, just like you, she'll stop eating or turn her head away."

I had to laugh. "Mom, did I turn my head away when I didn't want any more to eat?"

"Why does she cry so much, and kick her legs, and bite her arms?" slipped out of me. "Oops."

My mom put down the spoon and stopped feeding Joanie. She turned to me. Her eyes were a beautiful green and her smile so radiant. Her tender gaze seemed to linger much longer than usual. She gently touched my face and, in that moment, her whole attention was upon me. She wasn't in a rush, climbing the stairs from the basement after starting a new load of laundry, preparing a meal, washing the dishes, or putting another bandage on my knee. She was with me and I was with her. Her loving gaze filled me with a most wonderful sense of belonging. It doesn't matter now what she said in response to my frequent questions. But it surely did back then.

"She loves you and all of us, just as much as you love her. I can see how her pain affects you. I'm noticing you, too, you know! Your father and I would not want you or your brothers and sister to worry about her. You are very sensitive and notice so much."

She turned toward Joanie, who was keeping her gaze on us.

"Mom, what does Joanie really understand? Does she know what happened to her at birth? Does she understand why she has to be in a wheelchair? Does she feel so sad because she cannot walk or talk like we can?"

"My! You have so many important questions," my mother gently said. "There's so much that we don't know for sure about little Joanie. But every day I learn something new, and that helps me to care for her. I know now about what foods she likes and doesn't like."

"Yes, Mom, and she loves ice cream. I already know that!" I proudly stated.

Mom turned again toward me and continued. "I know that after three days she needs medication to help her tummy. When she starts to bite her hand, I know that she is in some kind of pain. That's when your father and I try to help her before her pain gets worse. A lot of times we think it's a really bad headache, so we have medicine for that."

Turing back toward Joanie, my mother gave her another large spoonful of eggs. Joanie loved eggs, just not early in the morning. Then Mom continued, "I know that when she cries and has a 'fit' in the middle of the night, it is so upsetting for all of us. It is so difficult to understand what is happening within her. We just stay with her, give her some special medicine, rub her back, and comfort her. The next morning, your father calls the doctor and lets him know, to see if there's anything more we can do."

"You know, sometimes when I'm with you and Dad to help hold Joanie down when she takes a 'fit,' I feel funny inside. I feel worried for Joanie. She can't even tell you where her pain is like I can when I'm in pain."

As Mom gazed lovingly upon me again, she said, "Yes, I completely understand. That's what happens in our hearts when we are with Joanie and she is suffering. Your heart hurts, too, because of your love for little Joanie."

Mom leaned over to me and gave me a big hug. "Now it's time for you to go out and play," she announced.

I jumped up and rubbed Joanie's shoulders. "Catch you later, Joanie," I told her. She smiled. As I ran out to the porch toward the front door, my mother said out loud, "Don't worry, Virginia, everything will be fine."

A few years later when we were enjoying a family vacation, I learned more about that kind of love. The best part was that Joanie was with us.

CONVERSATION WITH UNCLE VINNY

That summer, Uncle Vinny found a big, old, country house in Connecticut for us to rent for a month. It had plenty of bedrooms, so my grandparents and Uncle Vinny could come and stay, too. During those thirty days, a love for the country and joy of living so close to nature entered my soul and touched my heart forever.

The old home was located on ninety acres of grassy hills, just waiting for us to roll down, which we did! How I loved swimming and jumping into the lake from my dad's shoulders! There were fruit trees, raspberry bushes, and strawberry bushes to pick fruit from in the early morning for breakfast, just before the birds would swoop down and devour it all. I remember many antiques spread out over creaking wooden floors and old clocks standing like soldiers, guarding the passage of time.

> *A love for the country and joy of living so close to nature entered my soul and touched my heart forever.*

The country air offered a special and inviting fragrance, filled with the aroma of fresh-cut grass, baked just right from the afternoon sun, with a hint of tar from the newly paved country road. Each morning as I ran out through the screen porch door, whiffs of these fragrant earth's breaths greeted me. I felt at home in this enchanted place.

Fridays were special because Uncle Vinny would stay with us on the weekends after working during the week. I recognized the sound of his car's engine, his convertible DeSoto, as it approached. Jumping up with my lollipop in hand, stretching my gaze down the hill of the long and winding road, I'd listen. I was right!

"Uncle Vinny is here!" I would shout back to my siblings and they, in turn, relayed the news through the open windows with flowing curtains. Someone inside surely would hear our announcement: "Uncle Vinny is here!"

It would be years later before I heard the story of what happened during Uncle Vinny's visit. Each weekend, Uncle Vinny was able to observe how my mother, his sister, was so devoted to caring for Joanie. This care took up much of her day, and he saw no end in sight for this role and responsibility. He grew concerned for his sister.

"How can you possibly spend so much time with her, a person who cannot return any love?" Vincent asked out of great concern. My mother, who was giving Joanie a cold drink of juice, was taken by surprise. Considering this an opportunity, she turned and spoke calmly and directly.

"Listen, Vincent, I have something to tell you. God has put in my heart the same compassion that God has for little Joanie. I love her with that same amazing compassion. And by the way, Vincent, God loves you too!"

Imagine that! She was a carrier of God's incurable wound of compassion for so many, especially Joanie, Uncle Vinny, me, and my entire family. This gift and grace cannot be easily explained but are deeply felt. We read in John's Gospel of Jesus's desire for us to love in the likeness of God: "so that the love with which you have loved me may be in them, and I in them" (John 17:26). My mother was able to love in the likeness of God because, no doubt, she first experienced God's compassion for her. Mom was tiny but mighty!

Fr. William Barry, SJ, preached often about this ability to love as gift and intimacy with God. He called it "womb love" and wrote about it in his book *Experiencing God in the Ordinary*.[3] I heard him speak of this during a day of prayer, during which he also discussed his newly published book.[4]

During the day of prayer, Fr. Barry shared that the Hebrew word for *compassion* was related to the Hebrew word for *womb, rachamin*: "It is the kind of love a mother has when she risks herself for her child." Fr. Barry expressed that God shows such womb-love for us by risking God's self, especially through the passion and death of Jesus, for our salvation. As Fr. Barry communicated so often in his preaching and writing, God invites us to be God's image as friends and stewards in this world. God shows us how to live that way through Jesus. Little did we know that day of prayer would be Fr. Barry's last presentation, as he passed away just five months later. He devoted much of his ministerial life as a Jesuit priest to sharing about God's passionate desires and womb-love for all of us and all Creation. Fr. Barry was a carrier of God's incurable wound for others.

> *"God has put in my heart the same compassion that God has for little Joanie."*

My parents truly exemplified that womb-love of God, especially for little Joanie. Indeed, because of all the love that Joanie received from my parents and our entire family, she outlived all earlier predictions by doctors of her having a short lifespan. During their years of care, my parents filed papers to become Joanie's legal guardian and faithfully attended all her care meetings. After Joanie's placement in a state-run facility, we moved to be within five miles of her residence. That way my parents could continue to take Joanie home every other day. Joanie received the best of both worlds and much love. As time passed and my parents began to show signs of aging and were less able to keep up that ritual of care and accompaniment, I became more directly involved. My own commissioning hastened.

We are commissioned in so many ways. One way is by listening to the language of our souls and the desires of our heart. We will consider those invitations in the next chapter.

FOR REFLECTION

Recall time(s) when you experienced the compassion of God, or when you were a "carrier" of God's incurable wound of compassion for another. What was that like for you?

Chapter Six

LISTEN TO THE LANGUAGE OF OUR SOULS

You have kept count of my tossings;
put my tears in your bottle.
Are they not in your record?

Psalm 56:8

I have always been fascinated with languages. I greatly admire those who can speak several languages, while I struggled with Spanish and wish I had also learned Latin. My spelling would have improved! Learning other languages enables us to experience wonderful opportunities in meeting and communicating with others in our world. There are many languages to choose from. Yet, there is one not so well-known, and it is what I like to call the "language of our souls."[1]

God desires to communicate with us in many ways, including in the beauty of nature, in Scripture, in prayer and the sacraments, and in personal relationships. St. Ignatius of Loyola (1491–1556), founder of the Society of Jesus, was graced by God with the ability to articulate and write about his ongoing personal relationship with God.[2] Very briefly, Ignatius experienced a conversion that began during his participation in the Battle of Pamplona with the French (1521), during which time his leg was seriously injured by a big round pellet, much like a cannon ball. As his recovery was lengthy, he inquired about any available books to pass the time. He was offered two. One was on the life of Christ and the other was a collection of the lives of the saints. Ignatius would have preferred reading about stories of adventure, but he had no choice. While reading those spiritual books, he felt very inspired by the great sacrifices the saints offered to God and what they accomplished for God out of love. He began to imagine himself doing likewise, and perhaps even better. While he daydreamed of this new kind of dedication and devotion, he began to notice subtle but observable changes in his feelings, thoughts, and desires. Ignatius slowly recognized that God was speaking to him through those interior movements.

> The Holy Spirit helps and guides us to recognize which interior movements and choices are from God.

That was the beginning of a great grace from God and a radical change in his life. Ignatius would learn and teach others about the gift of discernment, which enables a person to better listen to the prompting of the Holy Spirit and to discover more of God's desires and invitations in the very reality of his or her life. It is a process whereby the Holy Spirit helps and guides us to recognize which interior movements and choices are from God and which are not.

Over the years as a Jesuit, St. Ignatius kept a journal of his experiences and of what seemed to be most helpful for others, along with insights, prayers, and suggestions. It became known as *The Spiritual Exercises of Saint Ignatius*.[3] In particular, St. Ignatius was able to identify and describe two of the most important interior movements as "consolation" and "desolation," which are part of the "language of our souls."

St. Ignatius describes consolation in his Spiritual Exercises: "When some interior motion is caused within the soul through which it comes to be inflamed with love of its Creator and Lord,…and every increase in hope, faith, and charity, and every interior joy which calls and attracts one toward heavenly things and to the salvation of one's soul, by bringing it tranquility and peace in its Creator and Lord."[4]

St. Ignatius describes desolation as everything contrary to consolation: "obtuseness of soul, turmoil within it, an impulsive motion toward low and earthly things, or a disquiet from various agitations and temptations. These move one toward a lack of faith and leave one without hope and without love."[5]

PERSONAL STORY OF DISCERNMENT

Early morning during one of my extended visits with my parents my father came back up the stairs holding an unopened can of coffee. Appearing to be confused and a bit distressed, he asked, "Virginia, can you help me?"

"Sure, Dad, what's up?" He scratched his head and looked up at me as he stood on the staircase.

"How do you open this can of coffee?" he said with a nervous laugh.

He always set up the coffee pot for all of us in the morning. By 7:00 a.m. the aroma drifted up slowly to the second floor. Standing before me was this brilliant engineer who designed navigational gyroscopes for Navy vessels and space craft, asking me early that morning, how to open a can of coffee. I was deeply moved and felt concerned.

"Come on, Dad," I reassured him. "Let's make the coffee together."

I handed him back the can of coffee just to see what he would do.

"You're supposed to connect this can with this electric opener. How do I do that?" he quickly asked.

After I just pointed in the direction of the electric opener, he said, "Oh yes, now I remember. I just need a little jump start sometimes." He shrugged his shoulders and smiled like a little boy.

I spent a lot a time with my father that day, not only to accompany him but also to observe a little closer. His memory was weakening. Before I left for my home and said goodbye to my mother, Dad came out to see me off. He hugged me and said, "I love you. Thank you for visiting again. You were a great help."

I noticed tears in his eyes when he also said, "I don't know what is happening to me. I feel like I'm losing control." That was one moment when I caught sight of him in his own suffering and worries.

Giving him a big hug, I said, "I love you, Dad. I'll be back soon." He smiled and began to wave as I drove back down the long driveway. As soon as I was out of sight, my own tears lined my cheeks. It was a long seven-hour drive home.

The next morning while sitting in my rocking chair and praying, I began to cry again and was unable to continue reading the Scripture passage of that day. I closed my prayer book and just sat there, no longer trying to stop my tears. Instead, I listened to my tears.

I felt as if God was inviting me to consider other possibilities in my life to better help my parents.

"Jesus, these words of Scripture are just bouncing off my head right now. I cannot concentrate. Be with me, Jesus,"

I prayed. Then I felt a moment of lightness and freedom within me. I continued talking with Jesus, as if he were sitting right next to me: "It was so hard to see my dad failing in health and having trouble with his memory. The look on his face when he told me he could not open the can of coffee touched my heart. It must have been so difficult for him to tell me he feels like he's losing control. He had always been in control in his life as he cared for all of us and Joanie. He could fix any problem with the house and our cars. He feels afraid right now.

"Jesus," I pleaded. "If there is any way that I can better help and accompany my parents right now in their need, please let me know. Let it happen." I sat in silence. Somewhere in the midst of my tears and prayers, I sensed an inner desire or encouragement welling up within. Then, I heard these words deep within: "Leave now! Just sell!" Leave now? Leave what? Sell what? Stocks? Furniture? I pondered.

It didn't take long to figure that one out. I felt as if God was inviting me to consider other possibilities in my life to better help my parents. That was my desire. Even though I was very involved with helping them, I realized that the seven-hour drives were challenging. Entering into a discerning process invites openness to the promptings of the Holy Spirit and leads to greater freedom. It is a process to carefully consider what additional choices are possible in response to our desires and the reality of the situation. Where is God inviting me? What is the greater good in the midst of all of my real, possible choices? That is at the heart of discernment.

As my discerning process continued, two viable options came into my awareness. *What if* I left my teaching position and engaged full time in ministry? (I had already received the necessary training and certification.) *What if* I sold my home and relocated to be nearer to where my parents lived? I was free to do both. Yet, it was a very significant change in my life.

I opted to leave my teaching position of many years and sold my home. My desire to accompany my parents during their time of need and the deep sense of compassion I felt for them were essential in this discernment process. I opted to make my decision from those perspectives, despite contrary advice related to the financial impact of my decisions.

The process of discernment often involves a heartfelt desire to discover the "greater good." That's what I wanted. Discernment is not a roadmap, but rather a trust walk with God. It is not a process to gain 100 percent assurance; yet, God does offer us confirmation. The authors of *What's Your Decision? How to Make Choices with Confidence and Clarity* say, "Knowing that we can trust our experience is the first, and perhaps the most fundamental, lesson about discernment."[6]

I received confirmation in several ways. However, it became most clear that my decision was a good one during my very next visit with my parents. Early one morning, my father rushed down the hallway and knocked on my bedroom door.

"Mom fell in the bathroom and I cannot lift her!" he anxiously called out. I rushed down the hallway and entered the bathroom. As I assisted my mother, I knew everything was about to change. I called 9-1-1.

The rescue squad arrived within minutes. So many emergency personnel entered our house and moved quickly up the stairs to help my mother. The two-way radio relayed loud messages full of static to a control center. The rescue squad requested an ambulance. Soon red flashing lights illuminated the driveway as I watched the EMTs strap Mom down on a gurney and carry her out to the waiting ambulance. A neighbor stayed with my father for a while so I could follow the ambulance to the hospital. I stayed by my mother's side through the whole process in the emergency room and the many hours of waiting for her admittance. At 1:00 a.m., she was finally transferred to a room and I could go home. When I arrived, Dad was still waiting up and noticeably anxious. I gave him a hug.

"Mom's going to be fine, Dad. She's finally in a room. They will take good care of her. Let's get some sleep."

This was a most difficult transitional time for my parents, as they had been very independent for so many years. With one fall, everything changed. They were fearful of the unknown, of changes, and how any change would impact them. Their biggest fear was having to leave their beautiful home, which to them would mean a total loss of control. It was. All I could do was to be with them and with my siblings, and help my parents make life-giving decisions.

Over the next few years, the transition progressed from having four hours of in-home assistance from an aide to having 24/7 live-in help. Yet, my parents still wanted their independence. After the very first home aide arrived at my parents' home and completed a full day's work, my parents fired her! Imagine that!

"We do not need your help. We are just fine here in our home. Thank you," my parents told the home care aide. Soon afterward, we engaged the services of a podiatrist who also offered home visits. Perfect! But when the doctor arrived and rang the bell, my parents would not let him in!

"We don't need any help with our feet," they called out to the doctor from the front door. "Thank you." The doctor left, and we were billed for his unsuccessful visit!

> *The most painful aspect was the imminent change of residency for my parents.*

One of my own worries soon came to be. When my father was in the hospital for a serious medical condition and my mother was at home with 24/7 care, it became more obvious that they needed more specialized care. To assist us in that process and decision, my siblings and I engaged the services of a health-care consultant.

The health-care consultant could arrange for any additional in-home evaluations necessary to acquire a PRI (patient review instrument) for any nursing home applications. She also was skilled in guiding us with finding the best match with available skilled nursing homes and navigating through medical insurance requirements. It's a most stressful process. Even when you find a good nursing home, you might be on a waiting list for several months. Of course, the most painful aspect was the imminent change of residency for my parents. Have you been there?

My parents were very aware that someday they may have to leave their home and take up residence in a skilled nursing home. They knew we were actively looking at possibilities for their care with the help of the health consultant. But actually doing it was entirely different.

How I enjoyed sitting outside with my mother in the warm afternoon sun enjoying a cup of tea. It was a quiet and peaceful time just to be together. While Silvia, our 24/7 home aide, was upstairs taking a much-needed break, Mom and I were discussing my father, following a serious medical situation and his placement in a hospital. We were anxiously waiting for an update on his status. The phone rang.

It wasn't a call from the hospital. It was from our health consultant, who was actively working on nursing home placements. When I finished the lengthy conversation, I knew I had to bring the news immediately to my mother about the sudden availability of rooms. Nursing homes fill beds quickly, so decisions needed to be made sooner rather than later. My siblings and I were all previously informed of the excellent quality of this particular nursing home. We all knew that when a call came in, we would have to respond immediately or lose the opportunity.

"Mom, that wasn't the doctor about Dad. It was the health consultant, the one trying to find a good nursing home," I said nervously. "There's good news and bad news," I continued. I was fully aware of this moment being so significant for both my parents. I wondered how she would respond. All I could do was to tell her the news and be with her.

Mom said, "Well, tell me the good news first," as she silently stared at me without any expression on her face.

"The consultant found a placement in an excellent skilled nursing home for Dad. So he can leave the hospital today and be transported this afternoon to receive the help he really needs," I carefully explained. "We are not able to care for him here at home," I said softly to my mom.

"Yes," she replied, "That does sound like good news. Now, what's the bad news?" Her arms stiffened as she braced herself in her wheelchair.

"The consultant was actually able to find a placement for you, too, at the same nursing home, Mom. That's almost impossible with the waiting list in nursing homes today. You will be able to be with Dad. Dad's too sick to come home here. But I'm so sorry, it means that you have to leave here, too," I said, holding back tears.

It felt like an eternity as I looked at my mother's unexpressive face. Was she in a bit of shock with this news? Our eyes were upon each other for an unbearable while. I wondered what was going through her mind and heart. "Mom, how are you?"

Finally, I heard her say, "Okay. Then let's go." It seemed like the sustained, tense silence fell in pieces around my feet. Looking intently at each other, I realized that we were never in this situation before. These were uncharted waters.

My heart was breaking for my mother. Her aide, Silvia, also seemed stressed. She stayed with my mother while I went up to her bedroom to pack some of her belongings. This would also mean that Silvia would be reassigned by her home-care agency.

A strained silence filled the car as I drove my mother to this nursing home. I never really expected this day to arrive. I tried for so long to help them stay in their home. As we drove farther and farther away from her beautiful home of forty years, my mother remained silent. I could only imagine how powerless she must have felt at that moment.

Never again would she open that front door. Never again would we sit outside on the front porch in the late afternoon sun. Never again would she welcome friends and family into her home. Asking seniors to make such radical changes in life is heartbreaking. The only consolation was that my parents' new residence would offer the specialized care they both needed. There were no other available options right now to best meet their needs. Her world, as she knew it, had dramatically changed again.

Upon arrival, Mom and I met with the social worker and began signing all the necessary paperwork for the admissions process. Then we were taken down the long hall to her newly assigned room. My mother remained silent as she viewed the stark cold walls without any familiar photos. It was not home, yet she knew she would be living in this nursing home for the rest of her life. While waiting for my father to be transported from the hospital, Mom began to cry. The reality was setting in.

"Please take me home. I don't want to stay here. I'm afraid." Mom was staring intently at me and her eyes were beginning to tear up. My heart was breaking, but I tried to comfort her. I felt like I was in the middle of a one-act play and that we would soon be able to return home. Not so.

"I don't know where I belong," she said with tears in her eyes. Those words pulled deeply within my heart—I understood her meaning. I put my arm around her. I was at a loss for words.

"You will always belong to Dad. You will always belong to me and our family." All I could do was hug her, and I felt a dreaded sense of finality. That was one of those times when compassion breaks your heart wide open and heavy suffering pours in.

"Let's just wait for Dad and see what happens. I'm with you, Mom." My mother agreed, but she looked distressed. My sadness deepened.

> *It was the place where Artie and Marie offered the same compassion of God to all who entered.*

Finally, after about three hours—it felt like an eternity—the ambulance arrived. They wheeled my father in on a gurney and brought him to a different room. As soon as possible, I took my mom down to be with him. She sat by his side, took his hand, and gazed lovingly upon him. From that moment, she never asked me again to take her home. They were together again in a new, unfamiliar residence. She knew where she belonged—with her husband, Artie.

My stomach ached and my tears were plentiful as I drove back home, leaving them for the first night in their new residence. They would live out the rest of their lives in that nursing home. It would also become a second home for me over the next fourteen years.

Driving up the long driveway, I knew no one would be there to greet me or share a meal. It would no longer be home again, nor the place of hospitality where our family had gathered for nearly fifty years. Those cherished memories were highlighted by my mom's homemade lasagna and chicken roll-ups! It was the place where Artie and Marie offered the same compassion of God to all who entered. A penetrating emptiness surrounded me, and tears flowed down my face as I sat in my father's favorite chair. Transitions can be so painful, even when decisions are made compassionately.

Over the next several months, my parents slowly acclimated to their new residence. Our family visits became familiar and comfortable at the nursing home. But as my father's medical condition worsened, the day arrived when he became weaker. One day he became unresponsive and passed away peacefully.

Mom immediately said, "He's been set free! Artie's set free. No more suffering!"

This blessed accompaniment with my parents began through the gift of tears and paying attention to the language of my soul. It is a language that embraces the desires of God with our desires and leads us deeper into the depths of compassion.

> Let nothing disturb you. Let nothing upset you.
>   Everything changes.
> God alone is unchanging. With patience all
>   things are possible.
> Whoever has God lacks nothing. God alone is
>   enough.
>
> St. Teresa of Avila, "Teresa's Bookmark"

FOR REFLECTION

Can you recall a time or moment when you recognized the "language of your soul"? How did that experience impact your life?

Chapter Seven

COMPASSION AND "BEING WITH"

When we are so moved by compassion for another in their need or suffering, sometimes the best response we can offer is to simply be with them. My mom slowly accepted her present reality and entered into her life in the nursing home, now without Artie. With openness of heart, she made new friends and began to enjoy again many of the activities available to her. I often accompanied her to activities and, when the weather was nice, we sat outside on the patio area. Afterward, I wheeled her around the long driveway and grounds to enjoy the beauty, the flowers, and the song of the birds. Life does simplify. It does come down to taking "one day at a time." What Mom taught me, especially during her residency in the nursing home, was to enjoy the present moment. It's the "being with" that matters the most.

"The hardest adjustment I had to make when coming to live in the nursing home was to learn how to wait," my mother shared with me. "No matter what you want or need, you can press the call button, but you have to wait. Sometimes an aide will come relatively soon. Most of the time, you have to wait and wait and wait. But I'm getting used to it. After I push the button, I try to think about something else to pass the time. What else can I do?"

My mother had several roommates after my father passed. Indeed, she lived there for twelve more years. Because of her kindness and joy to all, my mother became the "mayor" of the nursing home! Everyone knew her, and everyone loved her.

"You know," a nurse told me one day, "When a new resident enters the nursing home and they feel upset, we ask if he or she would like to speak to one of the residents. If they say they would, guess who we ask to help? Yes, of course, your mom, the mayor!"

> Because of her kindness and joy to all, my mother became the "mayor" of the nursing home!

Later, and with great delight, I said, "Why, Mom, you have a ministry!"

"I do?" She replied with an astonished and quizzical look.

"Yes, Mom, the nurse told me. What do you do, and what do you say to the new resident?"

"Well, I simply hold their hand, if they like. I tell them that this is a very good nursing home. Everyone will take good care of you. And the food's not so bad," she explained with a smile.

My mother did not isolate herself, especially after the passing of Artie. She continued being the same compassionate woman as she was in her life as wife, mother, sister, aunt, and grandmother. She was deeply moved when looking upon the anxiety or sadness of some of the residents. She would wheel herself around to visit and talk with anyone who seemed lonely or sad. She would just "be with them."

During one afternoon visit, we passed a resident who was sitting alone in her room and looking down at the floor. My mother gazed from a distance upon her and said, "I feel so sorry for her. She looks so lonely." My mother was no stranger to loneliness. As I said before, she was tiny but mighty! We both waved to the resident as we passed, and she smiled.

At ninety-six years of age, my mother's health began to decline. No longer did we move about freely in the nursing home or on the grounds, and my visits with her now were held by her bedside. With each passing day and week, she became noticeably weaker and was not eating. The very caring doctor clearly observed her decline and prepared my siblings and me for our mother's approaching death.

Because of her significant short-term memory problems, she would often repeat things: "What is happening to me?" "I'm not very hungry." "I feel so tired."

Each time I would gently answer her until the worry on her face lifted. "Mom, do you think that God is slowly calling you home?"

She would look at me and smile. "Yes, I guess so!"

I remember that late afternoon when I was sitting by her bedside. She appeared so tiny and weak. Then she looked over intently at me and said, "I'm afraid to die." I held her hand and stroked her beautiful face. Her sharing touched my heart as my gaze met hers.

"I understand, Mom. What are you most afraid of?"

"It's just so strange that we have to leave here and those we love. I don't know what it will be like, I mean the dying process. Once I get to the other side, I'll be okay!" she said effortlessly.

"I understand, Mom. There is nothing to fear. You are going from love to more love. Everybody loves you, Mom. God loves you. Artie loves you and is waiting for you." She looked up at me, nodded her head, and gave me a wink.

"All of the doctors here know what you are going through and are taking very good care of you. They are here to help you."

After some silence, she spoke. "Well, we all have to die someday, and no one can do it for you," she wisely observed.

"You're so right, Mom. I will surely remember that!"

"Besides, my old generation needs to 'jump ship' and let the next generation have more room," she said excitedly while lifting her arms up in the air.

"You are so beautiful, Mom. Don't worry about Joanie. We are all taking good care of her. Just rest now." Her eyes remained closed but she smiled. She heard me. While she rested, I stayed a bit longer just to continue to gaze upon her. I didn't want to be anywhere else. Then she began speaking, but too softly to hear. I heard her chuckling. Then she raised one of her arms and pointed up to the ceiling.

"Once I get to the other side, I'll be okay!"

When she noticed me still sitting by her side, she asked, "Did you see that woman with the hat? You used to work with her?" I had no idea, but just enjoyed my mom's sharing.

Over the next few days, I just sat by her side for hours whether she was sleeping or awake. She was no longer eating and was enrolled in "comfort care." My siblings all visited her when they were able. The nurses and doctors monitored her for any signs of increased pain, as they attended to her end stage of life. She was sleeping more and more and lying motionlessly in her bed. She was so quiet and required very little additional care.

The next day while I was sitting by her side, to my surprise, she gently awoke from her deep sleep. When she noticed me, her face lit up with a beautiful smile. All of a sudden, with increased energy, she spoke to me in a most loving way.

"It's so good to see you and thank you for being here. You are so good to me. You always think of others first." She continued to just speak gently, compassionately, and with great encouragement. I felt loved and ministered to from one so tiny and weak. But it was Mom, the one so full of kindness and compassion. In that moment, I received a most gracious and beautiful blessing from her heart.

As I was driving home and recalled my mom's words, I felt deep peace. Being with her was like being in God's presence. I remembered what she said years ago: "God put his compassion in my heart. I love little Joanie with the same love that God loves her." I felt as if my mother was loving me with the same love that God has for me. Her words were a great consolation, and I knew I would treasure that visit all my life. I didn't know it then, but those would be Mom's last spoken words to me.

That night, I wrote, "The night sky spread out in hues of deep purple, while stars were dancing so far above. Trains rumbling in the distance in rhymical clattering of steel, while carrying the late-night travelers. Jets soaring above while cars raced on the street below. A blessed day, being with her—in simple loving presence. These repetitive, evening, city noises screeching below. Life shouts out loud in some places. Yet, not so far away, within a deepening contrast of sacred silence, on a bed in a nursing home, my mom lies slowly dying."

When visiting her the next morning, she again appeared so tiny and motionless, and her complexion so very pale. This time, she remained asleep and unable to be awakened. The room filled with a reverent silence as my brother arrived to be with her, too. There was no more need of giving her any liquids. We just sat by her side. My words of love did not bring any changes to her face, nor a response, but I believed she could still hear us.

Will she wake up? I wondered. What is happening?

How does death come and take us away?

Later that morning, a nurse came in to give her the next dose of pain medication and stayed a bit longer with us. While I was holding my mother's hand and stroking her face, the nurse said tenderly to my brother and me, "I think your mom is leaving us."

My whole being came to attention. While gazing deeply upon her face, I, too, began to notice subtle changes in her complexion. She looked paler and a few blue lines were noticeable, and her body was absolutely motionless. She stopped breathing. It was true. Mom had passed in the most peaceful and gentle manner, in our presence, while I held her hand. Tears poured down my face.

How did she leave her tiny body? How does death come and take us away? Does her soul stay a little longer? Does she see me crying now? I interiorly questioned God.

"Mom, you are set free, just like Artie," I said through my unstoppable tears. "Thank you, Mom, for all of your love and compassion. No more suffering and no more fear or worries." My body released my vigil of tears, as I prayed by her side.

"God be with her. God be with us. God be with me and my siblings. I will miss you so much, Mom. Not to worry, I will take care of little Joanie"—I hoped she could still hear me. "We will all take care of little Joanie." She was rejoined with Artie. She was at peace.

Compassion and "Being With"

The late Cardinal Joseph Bernadine reflected about having peace of soul even as one nears death:

> Many people have asked me to tell them about heaven and the afterlife. I sometimes smile at the request because I do not know any more than they do. Yet, when one young man asked if I looked forward to being united with God and all those who have gone before me, I made a connection to something I said earlier in this book. The first time I traveled with my mother and sister to my parents' homeland of Tonadico di Primiero, in northern Italy, I felt as if I had been there before. After years of looking through my mother's photo albums, I knew the mountains, the land, the houses, the people.
>
> As soon as we entered the valley, I said, "My God, I know this place. I am home." Somehow, I think crossing from this life into eternal life will be similar. I will be home.
>
> What I would like to leave behind is a simple prayer that each of you may find what I have found—God's special gift to us all: the gift of peace. When we are at peace, we find the freedom to be most fully who we are, even in the worst of times. We let go of what is nonessential and embrace what is essential. We empty ourselves so that God may more fully work within us. And we become instruments in the hands of the Lord.[1]

Compassion is being with. God is with us in our lives and when we are called home. In the midst of our compassionate presence, we can receive and recognize special gifts to bless us on our journey. Let's consider these gifts in the next chapter.

FOR REFLECTION

Recall a time(s) when your "being with" another led to an experience of compassion. What was that like for you?

Chapter Eight

SPECIAL GIFTS FOR OUR JOURNEY

I became her advocate. I was her voice. Though completely dependent upon another for her well-being, her extraordinary life was immersed in mystery. What did she really know? How long would she live? What was she thinking? How did she feel?

Actually, no one could really know what it was like for my sister, Joanie, not even the doctors. She was born prematurely and remained unable to walk or talk throughout her entire life. She was diagnosed with cerebral palsy and was profoundly cognitively affected from complications during her birth. Yet, she lived with us as a family for about eighteen years before needing specialized care. She was loved. She loved all of us in her own way.

Being with my sister and loving her brought my family and me into intimacy with her joys and her pain and suffering.

Her suffering became our suffering. Yet, thank God, there were many good times.

In younger years, I discovered that Joanie especially enjoyed physical movement. One day, while sitting on the couch, holding her in my arms and rocking her back and forth, she began to laugh. Joanie liked the sensation of that movement. How wonderful to hear her laughter. One day while I was rocking her and she was laughing heartily, she began to call out, "Egga, egga, egga!" Incredible! Thinking that Joanie was actually talking, I ran into the kitchen to tell my mother.

"Mom, *Mom*, I was rocking Joanie, and she was laughing! Then, guess what, Mom? Joanie was talking! And, Mom, you won't believe this, but she wants eggs!"

My mother stopped whatever she was doing in the kitchen and put her arm around me. She told me that Joanie was not really talking, because she is not able to communicate in the same way as we can.

> *Joanie certainly outlived all of the previous predications of life expectancy.*

"She's just letting you know how happy she is to be with you," Mom explained. "I don't think she really wants eggs. She's just very happy and is vocalizing in the little way that she can. She's having fun with you."

Well, I went back into the living room and sat next to Joanie. She still had a silly look on her face. I whispered in her ear.

"Joanie, I believe you that you want those eggs! But listen to me Joanie. You're going to have to convince Mom if you really want those eggs!" I continued to rock Joanie back and forth and she continued to laugh. That was one of the happiest memories I have of Joanie.

Joanie certainly outlived all of the previous predications of life expectancy. It was because of all the love she received from our family; though I'm sure my parents never expected her to outlive them.

For as long as my parents were able, they cared for her in the most compassionate way. When their health declined and they took up residence in a skilled nursing home, I knew the baton needed to be passed. I initiated the process of transferring surrogate guardians from my parents to my siblings and me so that we could continue to make important medical decisions on her behalf.[1] Soon after that, I recognized Joanie's need for a M.O.L.S.T., or medical orders for life-sustaining treatment.[2] In that way, Joanie would live and die with dignity. The guardianship and M.O.L.S.T. applications were both involved and lengthy processes involving state agencies, the group home, and the nursing home. Gaining guardianship and the M.O.L.S.T. proved to be most essential and helpful for Joanie as she aged, and as her medical needs became more acute.

I felt blessed to accompany Joanie, especially during the last ten to fifteen years of her life, and did not want to be anywhere else. My siblings always remained very involved as well, but I was the one most free to be with her, especially for medical appointments, care meetings, and during any hospitalizations. We all loved Joanie and were committed to her well-being and quality of care.

Throughout my advocacy, I completed comprehensive notes and shared regularly with my siblings so that they were fully informed and knowledgeable of Joanie's medical situation. I knew Joanie, kept accurate observations of her patterns of pain and ease, and was able to communicate directly with staff and doctors. Many doctors particularly appreciated being able to view brief video clips that captured the key behavioral patterns of her pain, especially because Joanie was unable to speak for herself. During times when Joanie was admitted to the hospital, the medical doctors, who had no prior knowledge of her medical history or how she expressed pain, relied on my input. There were several critical medical appointments that I arranged for Joanie based on my observations. As a result, additional accurate medical diagnoses were made, which improved her overall quality of treatment and care. This was all a part of my ongoing advocacy for her.

> I received many gifts from Joanie.

After Joanie's fifth trip to the emergency room for the same medical issue one summer, it became obvious that she was in need of more specialized care. She was aging out of her present nonmedical residence in a state-run group home. This process required collaboration among the group home, state personnel, and nursing home administrators, and with our family. After visiting a few nursing homes and receiving guidance from a social worker, my siblings and I agreed upon a placement. This marked a most significant and important change for Joanie.

I felt immediate relief knowing that Joanie would now receive the appropriate medical care that she needed. However, it was still very important to stay involved simply because of Joanie's inability to communicate. My siblings and I were introduced to a new staff and new residents. I felt so grateful not only to all of the staff and nurses who cared so lovingly for Joanie on a daily basis, but also to many of the residents, who were so compassionate toward Joanie and became her friends. Realizing that she could not walk or talk, they would go out of their way to say "hello" and try to get her to smile. I enjoyed wheeling Joanie around on her floor so that we could connect more easily. Joanie brought out compassion in the hearts of those who came to know her. As time went on, everything settled down for a while. But by Joanie's second year of residency, she began to decline medically.

For a while, Joanie demonstrated repeated patterns of weakness and then would bounce back unexpectedly. She was a fighter, but soon she took another turn for the worse. Without really knowing when she would pass, we were aware that her time was approaching. My siblings visited to say good-bye and I connected my older brother via video chat so that he and his family had an opportunity to say good-bye, too. Joanie heard from all of us, which was so important to her. Then, at a time that God so desired, Joanie was released from her tiny body as she passed very peacefully and quietly. With a mixture of grief and relief for her, I cried while holding her tiny hand. Through my tears I said to little Joanie, "Thank you, Joanie, for being in my life. You taught me so much by your very presence. Your suffering opened up rivers of compassion in my heart. My life was in your hands. Thank you for all of your gifts. I trust I have become a better person because of you. I love you, Joanie. I will miss you so much. Be at peace with Mom and Dad."

As I look back over the years of my accompaniment with Joanie, the most difficult times were when I observed her to be in pain. Joanie received very good care and pain management in the nursing home, but often enough her behavior patterns strongly indicated that her pain continued. I completely understand the difficulties with pain management since Joanie was unable to communicate. As her advocate, I am highly trained in observational skills, well-read in the excellent research about identifying pain in a noncommunicative adult with developmental disabilities, utilized appropriate behavioral checklists for observations, kept brief video recordings of Joanie's behaviors, and knew Joanie all of her life. I had a moral and ethical responsibility to communicate my observations to the medical staff. There were times, despite my persistent advocacy, when I was told, "We do not see what you see. We do not interpret Joanie's behaviors in the way that you do."

My life was in your hands.

My sorrow penetrated to the depths of my being as I looked upon my sister in her silent suffering. I felt powerless against a powerful system. I sought help from the social worker to explore if there were alternative placement options for Joanie. Could she transfer into a different nursing home? Is she a candidate for hospice? Before I could even speak with my siblings about this concern, everything changed. As Joanie became frailer and weaker, we believed that her death was approaching, so a placement change seemed unnecessary at that time.

I remembered then what St. Paul of the Cross had taught and written about his experience of contemplation of Jesus's passion and death on the cross. He said there is no separation between the love and sorrow so deeply felt: "Rather love is permeated with sorrow, and vice versa, sorrow with love." Therefore, love and sorrow are "blended" or "mingled."[3] Since I was often with Joanie in her suffering, I experienced that mixture of sorrow and love with and for her.

We might experience the blending of sorrow with love at different times in our lives. Can you recall a time when you experienced this blending? Perhaps it was during a time you accompanied a loved one who was in hospice. Perhaps it was when you sat with a dear one who was receiving infusions for cancer treatment. Or you might remember when you cared for a loved one with Alzheimer's disease, when he or she no longer recognized you. Was your heart breaking with that blending of sorrow and love? God was with you.

As one unable to walk or talk, my sister profoundly influenced my life and the lives of so many. She was my greatest teacher. As a result, I received many gifts from Joanie. Here are my two favorite ones.

As a special education teacher for many years, I remember those rainy Monday mornings—filled with meetings and an abundance of paperwork. An attitude adjustment happened whenever I recalled the image of Joanie sitting in her wheelchair, which she was confined to for all of her life. Instantly, the well-known phrase captivated my mind: "Don't sweat the small stuff!"

We lose much psychological energy and inner peace when we engage in sweating the small stuff! Joanie inspired and reminded me often to simply let go of any small stuff and be grateful for all the many blessings I have received. Just being able to walk or run freely is a blessing. As I did so, my whole attitude would change, and I would have a great day, even on rainy Mondays! Thank you, Joanie!

The second gift that I have inherited from Joanie is what I like to call "anticipatory joy."[4] I have within the very marrow of my bones a vivid anticipation of when I will also be with Joanie in a place we call heaven. That anticipation became realized on August 18, 2019, when God so lovingly received Joanie home.

Now in her eternal life, I believe Joanie is able to walk and talk. That anticipation brings tremendous joy to me! We have a lot of catching up to do! I imagine when it is my time to go to God, Joanie will greet me. I often ponder: "What will her first words be for me?" Perhaps I will hear her laugh and say, "Where were those *eggs* I wanted?"

This gift of anticipatory joy is a very dynamic gift for all of us. This gift brings about a deep sense of gratitude for the many blessings we have received and helps us to keep our priorities in order. Thank you so much, Joanie!

God also wants us to have anticipatory joy of what lies ahead by God's desire for us and all of Creation. Without this anticipation, we can be more vulnerable to a darkness of diminished hope about our future or about any present suffering. We are also more vulnerable and perhaps more likely to view the world only through a lens of the predominant culture of our day.

We are a people of the *resurrection*—the beloved of God. We have a destiny and an invitation to co-participate in the continued emergence of the kingdom of God in our midst. This is a great source of hope for us and offers purpose and meaning in our lives.

> *"What will your first words to me be, my dear sister?"*

In some profound way, Joanie was just as much a part of God's loving plan as everyone else. She shared her gifts with us, and I, for one, was profoundly blessed. I wrote this letter after she passed:

EXPERIENCING GOD'S COMPASSION

My Dear Joanie,

This is my first letter to you in heaven. I was with you as you so gently, quietly, and peacefully left your tiny body in a moment that no one could have predicted. You were set free! I immediately imagined your wonderful reunion with Mom and Dad and all of our relatives and friends, followed by a grand tour of the cosmos led by Dad, and then an incredible welcoming celebration. Most profoundly, as Mom and Dad brought you face-to-face with God, you would have experienced the deepest, all-embracing love in ways that now fill me with deep peace and consolation. In that moment, you received complete awareness of who you were and are in God's presence, and of what happened to you in your birth and during your sixty-six years with us on Earth. I can picture you in full restoration of your mind and body and able to walk and talk. Imagine that! Did you dance and sing? What was that like for you, Joanie, when you came face-to-face with God? What was it like for you, Joanie, to be embraced by Mom and Dad?

One of my most heartfelt anticipations is when I can join you, as God desires! I long to see your face and hear your voice. What will your first words to me be, my dear sister? Surely, it will be a great reunion and joyful celebration.

Joanie, remember when Uncle Vinny questioned Mom about her ongoing care and devotion for you, when you were unable to return any love to her? Remember what Mom said to him in reply? She said, "Listen, Vincent, I have something I want to say to you. God has put compassion in my heart. I love little Joanie with the same compassion as God does. And, by the way, Vincent, God loves you too!"

I have come to believe that I have also received that tremendous grace. God put his compassion in my heart for you, just like God did with Mom and Dad. That was one of the greatest gifts I received from God, and you taught me how to receive that gift so I could accompany and advocate for you, as all of our siblings did, too.

So, dear Joanie, you now know everything about yourself in the light of God's eternal love. You know how much you were loved by all of us. You are now fully aware of your life's experience, whether it was of happiness and fun or of challenges and pain. You not only had all the medical challenges associated with cerebral palsy, since you could not walk or talk, but also the ongoing complications of the aging process. Of all of my cherished memories, those times when I could get you to laugh still bring me great joy.

Your suffering drew me into the depths of powerlessness that I have not experienced in any other way. Inside that powerlessness, all I could do then, Joanie, was to pray to God for help. I did that often while sitting by your side and holding your hand. We are now connected ever more by our mutual sharing in both suffering and joy.

I hope, Joanie, that my advocacy for you over the years, with all of the loving care of our entire family, made a difference in your life. My life was in your hands. Now, with great peace and joy, your life is fully and eternally in God's hands, and this is a tremendous consolation for me.

For one confined to a wheelchair all of your life and unable to walk or talk, I believe God has now bestowed upon you a special mission. Among other heavenly assignments, I trust you are now my advocate! Thank you, Joanie, so much. I love you.

In the next chapter, I will give attention to the kind of experience we can face in the midst of our compassionate actions and desires for the good. Have you ever felt an *emptiness* within your heart in the midst of your compassion? Let's explore this further.

FOR REFLECTION

Bring to mind any of the special gifts you received from a person who might have first appeared unable to bring such gifts to you. Take time to express your gratitude for that special person.

Chapter Nine

COMPASSION— SELF-EMPTYING LOVE AND THE POWER OF GOD

Let the same mind be in you that was in Christ Jesus, who, though he was in the form of God, did not regard equality with God as something to be exploited, but emptied himself, taking the form of a slave, being born in human likeness. And being found in human form, he humbled himself and became obedient to the point of death— even death on a cross. Therefore God also highly exalted him and gave him the name that is above every name, so that at the name of Jesus every knee should bend, in heaven and on earth and under the earth, and every

tongue should confess that Jesus Christ is
Lord, to the glory of God the Father.

Philippians 2:5-11

Have you ever felt an emptiness in the midst of loving and caring for others? It may be identified by some as "compassion fatigue." Yet, let's consider another possibility.

The Greek word *kenosis* describes the transformative process by which our life takes on more of the pattern of Jesus's passion, death, and resurrection in the midst of our compassion. *Kenosis* means "self-emptying" and expresses the kind of love that St. Paul speaks of in his letter to the Philippians. We, too, are called to love in a similar way, and this is a pure grace from God.

Filled with discouragement and sadness, we can erroneously think that we are moving away from God rather than closer. Here is a story that gives an example of this kind of loving, especially in our senior years. I invite you as you read to recall the many daily times in which you love in this way. God comes to our assistance and offers us encouragement.

A TINY KNOCK AT THE DOOR

During a time when I was invited to offer a year's consultation with a Community of Sisters, I also offered them a preached eight-day retreat. Just prior to the start of this retreat, one of the Sisters, whom I shall call Sr. Helen, approached me during lunch. Sr. Helen was the most senior member in the Community, a young ninety-two and all of five feet in height. She was a mighty one!

Sr. Helen told me that she wasn't sure if she would attend the retreat. She was convinced that she would not be able to hear me, pointing to her hearing aids.

"Well, Sr. Helen, why don't you come for the first session and sit right in the front and see how it goes?"

Looking right at me, she said, "I'll come to the first talk," and walked away. Sure enough, just as I was about to begin the retreat, Sr. Helen made her way down the center aisle to the seat in the front row, right in front of me. Once settled in, she kept her eyes glued on me throughout the whole presentation. Afterward, Sr. Helen came up to me with a great smile and declared, "I heard every word. I'll be back tomorrow!"

During the eight days of preaching, I also offered time for one-to-one conferences for spiritual conversations for anyone interested. About the third day into the retreat, while I was sitting in the conference room, I heard a faint knock on the door.

> "I feel I am disappointing my Sisters. I feel
> I am disappointing God, too."

"Come in," I said. The door opened slowly and Sr. Helen appeared at the entrance of the room. At first sight, she looked very tired. The weight of the world seemed to be on her shoulders. Slowly, she entered and sat down. Silence. Then she looked up at me and said, "I didn't think I would come in to see you. I feel very sad," as she pointed to her heart. Her head leaned downward and her face wrinkled with worry. We began conversing and I encouraged her to speak more about her sadness.

"I used to be able to do a lot of work here. I'm ninety-two, you know!" She said proudly. "But now, all I can do is take care of the dog and water the plants. I feel I am disappointing my Sisters. I feel I am disappointing God, too. And I really cannot pray the way I used to." Then pointing to her heart, she said, "I feel very sad here. I carry this sadness around all day. It never leaves me."

As I listened to Sr. Helen share her experiences, compassion welled up within me. Since being with the Sisters for the year's consultation work, I had opportunities to get to know them. When I joined them for meals, I enjoyed hearing stories about their life. I also heard many wonderful stories about Sr. Helen.

She left her homeland as a teenager to come with her Community to the United States and establish this Community location. In the beginning years, Sr. Helen was very strong and was responsible for the management and care of the farm and the animals.

"You know, when I first arrived here, I couldn't speak much English. But it really didn't matter much because I took care of the farm and the animals. They understood me very well," Sr. Helen said proudly. "It was hard work, though.

My God, the huge boulders that I had to dig out of the soil took several days. But that was my work for the day. It was good work," she happily declared as she raised her hands upward in reverence to God.

"Sr. Helen, how amazing! I am so interested in hearing more about your early experiences."

"Well," she said, "You know I could really write a book! We used the boulders to form the stone walls and to make some separate places for the animals to graze. We had a big barn and a lot of animals. I named my favorite cow Betsy! Let me tell you, she had a mind of her own. One afternoon, Betsy somehow slipped out of the barn and started running down the middle of Main Street!" Her face lit up with excitement and her hands became animated as she shared her story.

Sr. Helen continued, "I had no other choice but to go running after her!"

"I would have loved to have seen you running down Main Street after Betsy!"

"I'm not really able to do much work now."

Sr. Helen quickly responded, "You and a whole lot of other people. A lot of our neighbors were standing on the side of the road laughing. I didn't think it was very funny at the time. I may have been very short, but I could run fast back then. I caught up to Betsy and turned her right around, and we headed back to the barn."

Then with a twinkle in her eye, she said, "I had to give a stern warning to Betsy not to ever do that again!"

"Sounds like you have had a very busy and hardworking life, Sr. Helen. I can see how you also really enjoyed your work." She was appearing to be more relaxed and less sad.

She chuckled nervously. "Yes, those are wonderful memories. That's why I think I feel so sad now. Some days I just can't shake it. I'm not really able to do much work now. The other Sisters have to do all the work. The worst part is when I feel I am disappointing my Sisters and even disappointing God. It's hard for me to be hopeful about my life."

Sr. Helen's expression changed, and she looked so visibly sad and tired. Her eyes were downcast, and she took in a slow deep breath. She reached down on her right side and began to hold sections of her long rosary beads. The metallic clicking noise pushed the silence between us away.

I became aware that sitting across from me was this wonderful and generous, seasoned Sister, who dedicated her life to helping others. She lived a life of compassion. What could I possibly say to help her? What would God want to say to this precious one? I pondered.

"This is why I feel so empty inside," she slowly stated. I sat in silence with her while I prayed to God for inspiration. After a few moments, I asked her a question.

"Have you told Jesus how you feel?"

"What?" Sr. Helen sat up attentively in her chair.

"Have you told Jesus about your sadness and your emptiness?" I repeated.

"Well, no! He knows everything, so he already knows that, right?"

"Yes, truly he knows. Yet, it's most helpful when we share this truth with him just as you have done with me. It's the same as when we want to deepen in our intimacy with anyone. The personal sharing, especially of our feelings, is so important. Then our prayer becomes more dynamic. This is one way in which we grow in intimacy with Jesus and allow Jesus to help us. Would you like to speak this way with Jesus?"

After a little pondering, Sr. Helen looked up and said, "I will at least try it. I thought he knew all of this. But I will tell him just like I told you. I never really remember praying this way. I think I will feel a little awkward." Sr. Helen nervously moved her rosary beads in her hands.

I offered more encouragement for this way of praying. "Just see what happens."

"I will. Just as you've encouraged me to do. Thank you so much. God bless you!"

She got up to leave. "I have to go water the plants and walk the dog!" Sr. Helen proudly announced.

The Community retreat continued. Then, about two days later, there was a stronger knock upon my door.

"Come in." Sr. Helen appeared in the open doorway. Her whole countenance was so markedly different. She appeared full of energy and her smile lit up the room. She came in and sat down in the same chair as before.

"I just wanted to come by and thank you," she quickly said. "I did what you suggested. It was a little awkward at first because I never really prayed that way before. But I told

Jesus about my sadness and my emptiness." Now she was confident.

She paused a moment before looking directly at me. It was as if she really wanted my attention. "And do you know what Jesus said to me about my sadness and emptiness?" she asked eagerly.

"What did Jesus say to you?" I responded enthusiastically.

"Jesus said that my emptiness is *not* emptiness. He said that my emptiness is fullness!" She lifted her arms up high again in reverence. Her voice was strong and her face so animated. I thought she was going to jump right up from the chair.

"I really felt his presence in a most loving way. Jesus seemed to understand my sadness even in my old age. He does not want me to be disappointed because he said I was loving just like he loves. Can you image that? Everything is going to be okay. I feel very relieved. Even my sadness is gone!"

"Jesus said that my emptiness is fullness!"

She continued to speak of her prayer experiences with Jesus. We took some time to just pray together in gratitude to God. Then, as Sr. Helen was leaving, she stopped in the doorway and turned around. "Thank you again so much. I feel better knowing I haven't disappointed God or my Sisters! Now I can die in peace!" she declared.

As I watched this precious one walk slowly down the long convent corridor, peace filled my whole being and tears of gratitude to God welled up in my eyes. I knew I was in the presence of a holy woman of great compassion. I thanked God for Sr. Helen.

Sr. Helen was given a great grace by God. Perhaps she was searching for the God of her youth in her old age. She was measuring her worth by the quantity of work rather than by the quality of her ministry and of her presence. She discovered that.

She invited Jesus into the present reality of her life. Through her honest and personal sharing with Jesus in prayer, Sr. Helen came to realize that her feeling of emptiness was not an indication of emptiness but of fullness. Her self-emptying love resembled the way in which Jesus loved. She received peace and she sensed a deepening in intimacy with Jesus. It was like a homecoming.

Our whole life is a prayer. Yet, we can, like Sr. Helen, become sad and discouraged when we have poured ourselves out so compassionately for others. Parents, grandparents, teachers, medical professionals, caregivers, just to name a few, all can witness to this kind of loving embraced within compassion. But then, there can be a time when we feel empty. We might then question and doubt ourselves, especially in our senior years when we look back at our lives. We can misperceive our experience of emptiness when we are loving so compassionately and erroneously believe that the accompanying sadness is a sign that we did not do enough. Those thoughts are not from the Holy Spirit!

Rather than consider our normal aging process as a diminishment, we can better imagine our aging process more from God's perspective. God desires to give us peace and consolation throughout our life, and especially in the midst of our seasoned years. Indeed, we can come to discover that "all human growth is in fact a growing participation in divinity."[1]

A friend and spiritual guide, Fr. Fidelis, once shared his belief that since Jesus lived to be thirty-three, he never experienced the significant challenges and sufferings of growing old. Jesus was not confined to a wheelchair, nor did he use a walker or cane. He did not experience memory loss or dementia. This is not in any way to attempt to compare Jesus's pain with the pain we suffer as we age. Rather, Fr. Fidelis suggested that this is an invitation.[2] As we bring our experiences of aging into conscious awareness and into our prayer, we can offer ourselves in this reality to God. In faith, we can believe that God will incorporate our present suffering into the mystical Body of Christ. This mystery is expressed well in Colossians: "I am now rejoicing in my sufferings for your sake, and in my flesh I am completing what is lacking in Christ's afflictions for the sake of his body, that is, the church" (1:24).

Our aging process is a sacred self-donation unto God. Can we believe that we are "completing what is lacking in Christ's afflictions for the sake of his body, that is, the church"? When we willingly offer our experiences of our senior years, God can lovingly accept and incorporate those experiences into the ongoing progression of the mystical Body of Christ.

In our senior years, this self-emptying encompasses our entire being.

I remember a time when Fr. Fidelis was visiting a senior man named Frank, who was in the process of dying. This man's wife and children were there, and they were deeply saddened and distressed. Fr. Fidelis spoke privately with Frank and helped him to see that even in his dying process, he could find a way to lovingly teach his family. Fr. Fidelis invited Frank to witness to his family about how to die in the midst of this great unknown. This invitation gave Frank a new purpose in his last days. Frank's death became a gift of self-donation and *kenosis* back to God, and a loving witness for his family.

So it is that spiritual luminary Pierre Teilhard de Chardin, SJ, prayed,

> When the signs of age begin to mark my body (and still more when they touch my mind); when the ill that is to diminish me or carry me off strikes from without or is born within me; when the painful moment comes in which I suddenly awaken to the fact that I am ill or growing old; and above all at that last moment when I feel I am losing hold of myself and am absolutely passive within the hands of the great unknown forces that have formed me; in all those dark moments, O God, grant that I may understand that it is you (provided my faith is strong enough) who are painfully parting the fibers of my being in order to penetrate to the very

marrow of my substance and bear me away within yourself.[3]

Our gift of self in seasoned years is no less important or less cherished by God than in the days of our youth. The days of our youth are just the beginning of a life characterized by self-emptying love. Throughout our lives, our experiences of *kenosis*, or self-emptying love, are God's way of loving, and are not only transforming for us but for those we love and for our world.

Yet, God's compassion is more embracing still. In the next chapter, we will turn attention to how all Creation mediates God's compassion, sometimes in surprising ways.

FOR REFLECTION

Think of times when the way you loved others was "self-emptying love." What was happening in your life and in your heart?

Chapter Ten

GOD'S COMPASSION WITH AND THROUGH OUR EARTH-HOME

The heavens are telling the glory of God; and
the firmament proclaims his handiwork.

Psalm 19:1

God desires our happiness. That desire cannot be sepa-
rated from the appreciation, enjoyment, and care of
all Creation. The very well-being of our lives is intricately
and intimately connected with life on Earth. Pierre Teilhard
de Chardin, SJ, said, "There is a communion with God, and
a communion with Earth, and a communion with God
through Earth."[1]

As we have reflected much upon God's compassion
for us, let's consider in this last chapter two true stories of
how God's compassion through our Earth-home can bring

about much healing and peace. Think of a time when Earth's beauty captured your heart!

All Creation was created by God, and "God saw everything that he had made, and indeed, it was very good" (Gen 1:31).

THE STORY OF THE BROKEN LEAF

Thomas was a man with a mission. He had always been highly successful in his academic studies all of his life. In fact, he had always received *A*s. He breezed through school and then began studies to become a nurse. He had a great desire to help others. Again, he excelled in all of his classes, received his diploma, and embarked on this new and rewarding career.

After completing a few years as a nurse in a large hospital, he was encouraged to become a supervisor. With that wonderful encouragement and affirmation, he researched available programs and enrolled in a PhD program near where he worked.

Time passed quickly and Thomas found himself fully immersed in studies for final exams and for his oral dissertation. Because he had devoted so much of his time to this study and preparation, he felt confident about the outcome. Much to his great surprise and astonishment, he received notice that he had failed both! Thomas was heartbroken. He began to isolate himself and grew increasingly despondent. He even refused to see his friends. This was his first experience of failure.

"Would you like to buy a leaf?"

"I'm no good. I'm a failure. I should never have begun this program in the first place," Thomas bemoaned. There were no signs of improvement for several months, until the dawn of a beautiful crisp, autumn day. Thomas felt spontaneously drawn to go outside his apartment for a walk and for some fresh air. He couldn't remember the last time he felt the sun or the breeze on his face. During his walk, and without noticing, he came upon a most ambitious young girl. She had set up a small table by the park's nature walk with a prominent sign: "Autumn Leaves for Sale."

As Thomas approached her table, she inquired, "Would you like to buy a leaf? They only cost a penny!" She gazed curiously upon this man with disheveled hair.

"Well, I would like to, but I do not have any money with me. I just left my apartment without my wallet." He hoped this explanation would excuse him from any further conversation.

"Oh, that's okay," she said. Then reaching into the very bottom of the bowl of available leaves, she pulled out a broken leaf. "Here!" She stretched out her hand. "This one is for you. It's for free!" she proclaimed with a beautiful smile.

Awkwardly, but without hesitation, Thomas moved slowly toward the little girl's table with the big bowl of autumn leaves. As he caught a glimpse of her eyes upon him, he thought, "So much kindness in one so young."

He very gladly received the gift of the free, broken leaf. "Thank you very much. This leaf is truly beautiful!"

"Yes," the little girl enthusiastically replied. "Don't you just love autumn leaves? They take my breath away!" She flung her arms and hands upward toward the expansive blue sky.

> *"That girl looked at me with the kindest expression, which deeply touched my heart."*

Thomas continued on his walk, now with the gift of a broken leaf in his pocket. The sun gleamed strongly through the trees as the leaves seemed to dance in the chilled air. Thomas felt more peaceful than he had in a while and headed back to his apartment. When he sat down on the couch and examined the broken leaf more closely, he broke down and cried. With that, everything changed! He immediately called his closest friend.

Tears continued to accompany Thomas as he spoke. "I wish you were with me, Kate," Thomas said with a shaky voice. "I never experienced anything like this. A young, entrepreneurial girl set up a table to sell autumn leaves." As Thomas continued to share his experience, he stopped in the middle of a sentence. "Kate, that girl looked at me with the kindest expression, which deeply touched my heart. It's like a cement block was removed from deep within. My shoulders even feel less tense. It was so evident that those beautiful leaves brought her joy. Imagine that!"

Soon afterward, Thomas rediscovered his own desire for nursing and reenlisted in that PhD program. With continued dedication and study, Thomas passed all final exams and his dissertation with flying colors. He became a very successful and beloved nurse supervisor.

That young girl, filled with an infectious love of Creation, shared a broken leaf and Thomas's life changed. He more easily reasoned that it is okay to fail. With that resilient message from the broken leaf, Thomas came to realize that his need for perfection in everything prevented him from experiencing brokenness as a grace, because it can lead us to reach out to others and to God. Thomas was set free.

Can we consider that a broken leaf from a child was a grace from our compassionate God through Creation? The grace and love of God can be revealed to us in infinite ways and can take us by surprise. How important to remain open to the surprises of God and the messengers that God may be sending to us on any given day. God shares of his love through the beauty of Creation for our healing, well-being, and enjoyment.

A HEALING ENCOUNTER THROUGH CREATION

I will now allure her, and bring her into the wilderness, and speak tenderly to her.

Hosea 2:14

I remember a time when my heart was broken and God's compassion was the very source of my healing through the gift and beauty of Creation. After the sudden, tragic death of Jack, the person I loved and had hoped to marry, I realized that I was losing hope. My friends were concerned and knew I needed to get away. They planned a special trip out to the Grand Canyon and invited me to join them. Initially, I turned down their invitation, as I really had little interest in travel at all. For that matter, I had little interest or energy in or for anything. Luckily, their persistence convinced me. I set out across the country with my dear friends, not realizing what would happen to me.

My healing actually began during our descent on the trails of the Grand Canyon. About halfway into our seven-hour downward hike, the very tiny trails that were hugging the Canyon walls suddenly opened up upon a vast plateau. As I traversed this expanse and felt the great warmth of the sun and power of the wind, I sensed God's loving presence.

> *The grace and love of God can be revealed to us in infinite ways and can take us by surprise.*

I became immersed in this exquisite grandeur. Stretching out my arms and looking upward into the windswept, blue sky, I shouted, "Hello, Creator God!" I remained still, silent, and attentive. My whole being was captivated by such beauty and presence.

I also felt completely powerless! All power belonged to God in this glorious place. My attention shifted away from myself and my broken heart and was drawn toward the immense beauty surrounding me. I felt lifted up and released from the previous burden of my broken heart. God used the beauty of Creation not only to get my attention but to invite me into a healing process.

The walls of the canyon seemed to gleam and dance in the afternoon light. The wind now carried—so it seemed—my broken heart's silent grief upward, like incense. I wasn't fully aware of my healing until I rejoined my friends and delighted in listening to their many stories. A significant sign of healing was when I began laughing again while enjoying their good company. Laughter had left me for a long time.

The deeper my descent into Earth's ancient-walled trails, my own awareness of brokenness and need for healing grew. God visited me in this canyon, while the wind-borne sunlight streamed and danced wildly upon the canyon walls! God's personal love and compassion for me was at the very center of my healing. In that moment, in the depths of the Grand Canyon, everything changed for me.

At different times in our lives, we experience brokenness and we suffer. Death takes our loved ones away. We grieve. We weep. We seek understanding in the midst of such sorrow. We need to be held. We need to reconnect with love. Most profoundly, as I discovered that day, the very experience of God's personal, loving compassion is at the heart of our healing and freedom, and it enables us to reclaim our lives. God finds us in the very reality of our lives, even through the gift and beauty of Creation. Psalm 139:6 says, "Such knowledge is too wonderful for me; it is so high that I cannot attain it."

I had the privilege of speaking one day with John Surette, SJ, author of *The Divine Dynamic*. He reflected on the intertwining of relationships with our Creator and all Creation, including with other people and with Earth: "We live within a unity of Divine-human relationship, with human-human relationship, and with our Earth-human relationship. Indeed, there is no separation between those relationships, as the spiritual and the physical are two dimensions of the single reality."[2]

FOR REFLECTION

Recall a time when your heart was captivated by a moment with Earth's beauty in Creation. What was that like for you? How did that experience impact your life?

EPILOGUE

I wrote this book during the first year of the global COVID-19 pandemic. Certainly, this pandemic has significantly impacted not only our present but also our future. Every aspect of our lives has been affected.

With the requirements to stay at home, I desired like so many to do something purposeful and meaningful. Much was transpiring at that time in my life, in this country, and in the world. While a highly contagious virus spread rapidly and brought death and havoc to millions of people, our country also witnessed protests and marches for social and racial justice. Suffering was everywhere and compassion was so desperately needed.

Looking forward through the lens of compassion, having reflected on these stories and Scripture, where does hope lie? What do you long for in your future for yourself, family, friends, church, our world, and our Earth-home? Is our compassion, flowing from God's womb-love (*rachamin*) for us, a pathway forward in the midst of all the suffering? I leave you with this hopeful, poetic invitation from Fr. Pedro Arrupe, SJ:

Nothing is more practical than finding God, that is, than falling in love in a quite absolute final way. What you are in love with, what seizes your imagination, will affect everything.

It will decide what will get you out of bed in the morning, what you do with your evenings, how you spend your weekend, what you read, who you know, what breaks your heart, and what amazes you with joy and gratitude.

Fall in love, stay in love, and it will decide everything.[1]

NOTES

PREFACE

1. Henri Nouwen was a priest of the Archdiocese of Utrecht, the Netherlands. He was a prolific writer, especially on topics related to compassion. Quoted from *Compassion: A Reflection on Christian Life* by Henri J. M. Nouwen, Donald P. McNeill, and Douglas A. Morrison (New York: Doubleday, 1982), 4. In his later years, he lived at L'Arche Community Daybreak in Toronto, Canada.

2. William A. Barry, "God's Sorrow: Another Source of Resistance?" *Review for Religious* 48, no. 6 (November–December 1989):842, 843.

CHAPTER ONE

1. Francis Thompson, "The Hound of Heaven," in *Poems* (London: Merrie England Publication, 1893).

CHAPTER TWO

1. His Holiness the Dalai Lama, *Toward a True Kinship of Faiths: How the World's Religions Can Come Together* (New York: Doubleday, 2010), 129. He has said that his first teacher of kindness and compassion was his mother.

2. John R. Donahue, *The Gospel in Parable: Metaphor, Narrative, and Theology in the Synoptic Gospels* (Minneapolis: Fortress Press, 1988).

3. Donahue, *The Gospel in Parable*, 153.

4. Donahue, *The Gospel in Parable*, 154.

5. William A. Meninger, *The Process of Forgiveness* (New York: Continuum Press, 1997), 37.

6. Nelson Mandela was the first Black president of South Africa, elected following imprisonment for his antiapartheid work. He won the Nobel Peace Prize in 1993.

7. Meninger, *The Process of Forgiveness*, 30.

8. N. T. Wright, *Evil and the Justice of God* (Downers Grove, IL: Intervarsity Press, 2013), 135.

9. Peter van Breemen, SJ, *The God Who Won't Let Go* (Notre Dame, IN: Ave Maria Press, 2001), 127.

10. Archbishop Desmond Tutu, *No Future without Forgiveness* (New York: Doubleday, 2000), 259; a South African Anglican cleric and theologian, known for his commitment and work for human rights.

CHAPTER THREE

1. I have used the term *resurrection dynamic* to describe an action of God within us through the gift of Jesus's resurrection, for any aspect of our healing and empowerment.

2. I have used *unresurrected powerlessness* to describe a process of transformation of God's grace as we move through our powerlessness into a place of healing.

3. I have used *resurrected powerlessness* to describe the impact of God's grace within us as we proceed through our experience of powerlessness into a more mature faith relationship, characteristic of the invitation found in 2 Cor 12:9–10 (God's grace is made perfect in weakness: "For whenever I am weak, then I am strong").

Oftentimes, this occurs when we receive grace that "elevates" us through the virtues of faith, hope, and charity.

4. William A. Barry, *God's Passionate Desire and Our Response* (Notre Dame, IN: University of Notre Dame Press, 1993), 25.

5. Richard Rohr, OFM, "Online Daily Meditations," March, 23, 2020, Center for Action and Contemplation, https://cac.org/daily-meditations/.

6. John O'Donohue, *Eternal Echoes: Celtic Reflections on Our Yearning to Belong* (New York: Harper-Collins, 1999), 144.

CHAPTER FOUR

1. I have used the term *incurable wound*, as found in Scripture, to describe an aspect of God's unconditional love for us.

2. William A. Barry, *God's Passionate Desire and Our Response* (Notre Dame, IN: University of Notre Dame Press, 1993), 842–43.

3. Richard Rohr, OFM, "Online Daily Meditations," March, 23, 2020, Center for Action and Contemplation, https://cac.org/daily-meditations/.

4. Robin Ryan, *God and the Mystery of Human Suffering* (Rockville, MD: LEARN25, 2011), Twelve-Part CD Set.

5. Rumi, *Love: The Joy That Wounds; The Love Poems of Rumi* (repr., London: Profile Books, 2017).

6. St. John of the Cross, *Dark Night of the Soul*, trans. E. Allison Peers (New York: Image Books, 1959), Stanzas 5, 7–8.

7. Terence E. Fretheim, *Jeremiah* (Macon, GA: Smyth and Helwys Publishing, 2002), 15:9.

8. Terence E. Fretheim, *The Suffering of God: An Old Testament Perspective* (Philadelphia: Fortress Press, 1984), 109.

9. Fretheim, *The Suffering of God*, 116.

10. Fretheim, *The Suffering of God*, 123.

11. Fretheim, *The Suffering of God*, 124.

12. Abraham J. Heschel, *The Prophets, Volume II* (New York: Harper and Row, 1962), 4.

13. Heschel, *The Prophets, Vol. II*, 89.

14. Heschel, *The Prophets, Vol. II*, 3.

15. Heschel, *The Prophets, Vol. II*, 11.

16. Robin Ryan, CP, *God and the Mystery of Human Suffering*, Audio CD (Rockville, MD: LEARN25, 2011), www.learn25.com.

CHAPTER FIVE

1. Robin Ryan, *Gazing on His Face: A Christ-Centered Spirituality* (Mahwah, NJ: Paulist Press, 2020), 101.

2. Cerebral palsy describes a medical condition that affects physical movements, muscle tone, and posture. Believed to be caused by damage to the developing brain before birth, the severity determines the extent of impairment to all aspects of a person's physical and cognitive abilities.

3. William A. Barry, SJ, *Experiencing God in the Ordinary* (Chicago: Loyola University Press, 2020), 47.

4. "Day of Prayer" at Campion Conference and Renewal Center in Weston, Massachusetts, held via Zoom, was about Fr. William Barry's *Experiencing God in the Ordinary*. During this presentation on July 19, 2020, Fr. Barry spoke of God's love for us as "womb love."

CHAPTER SIX

1. I have used the term *language of our souls* to communicate the various interior movements that can be experienced within a process of discernment.

2. St. Ignatius of Loyola was the founder of the Society of Jesus (1491–1556), also known for his gift and sharing of discernment in *The Spiritual Exercises of Saint Ignatius*.

3. Ignatius of Loyola and George E. Ganss, SJ, *The Spiritual Exercises of Saint Ignatius: A Translation and Commentary* (Chicago: Loyola Press, 1992), 122.

4. Ignatius of Loyola and Ganss, *The Spiritual Exercises of St. Ignatius*, 122.

5. Ignatius of Loyola and Ganss, *The Spiritual Exercises of St. Ignatius*, 122.

6. J. Michael Sparough, Jim Manney, and Tim Hipskind, *What's Your Decision? How to Make Choices with Confidence and Clarity* (Chicago: Loyola Press, 2010), 39.

CHAPTER SEVEN

1. Joseph Cardinal Bernardin, *The Gift of Peace: Personal Reflections* (Chicago: Loyola University Press, 1997), 152, 153.

CHAPTER EIGHT

1. Surrogate guardians can also be known as "health-care proxy" for those who are not able to make medically related decisions for themselves.

2. M.O.L.S.T. (Medical Orders for Life-Sustaining Treatment) allows for the improved quality of life for those who are seriously ill or near the end of life. The information in the M.O.L.S.T. contains the person's present health status, prognosis, and goals for care (to ensure these are honored by one's medical health professionals).

3. Martin Bialas, *The Mysticism of the Passion in St. Paul of the Cross* (San Francisco: Ignatius Press, 1990), 201.

4. I have used the term *anticipatory joy* to describe how an anticipation of a future joy can directly impact us in the present moment.

CHAPTER NINE

1. Daniel A. Helminiak, *Spiritual Development: An Interdisciplinary Study* (Chicago: Loyola University Press, 1987), 183.

2. Fidelis Connolly, CP (1921–2014), retreat master and preacher with the Passionist Community of St. Paul of the Cross Province.

3. Pierre Teilhard de Chardin, SJ, "Prayer of Diminishment," in *The Divine Milieu* (New York: Harper and Brothers, 1960).

CHAPTER TEN

1. Pierre Teilhard de Chardin, SJ (1881–1955) was a French Jesuit priest, scientist, paleontologist, theologian, philosopher, and teacher.

2. From an interview with Fr. John Surette, SJ, in May of 2021. See his book *The Divine Dynamic: Exploring the Relationships between Humans, Earth, and the Creative Power of the Universe* (Chicago: Acta Publications, 2010), 8.

EPILOGUE

1. Pedro Arrupe, SJ (1907–1991), was from the Basque region of Spain and served as the 28th Superior General of the Society of Jesus.

Appendix

RESOURCES

BOOKS

Aschenbrenner, George A., SJ. *Stretched for Greater Glory: What to Expect from the Spiritual Exercises*. Chicago: Loyola Press, 2004.

Barry, William A., SJ. *Praying the Truth: Deepening Your Friendship with God through Honest Prayer*. Chicago: Loyola Press, 2012.

———. *Changed Heart, Changed World: The Transforming Freedom of Friendship with God*. Chicago: Loyola Press, 2011.

———. *A Friendship Like No Other: Experiencing God's Amazing Embrace*. Chicago: Loyola Press, 2008.

———. *Letting God Come Close: An Approach to the Ignatian Spiritual Exercises*. Chicago: Loyola Press, 2001.

———. *Paying Attention to God: Discernment in Prayer*. Notre Dame, IN: Ave Maria Press, 1990.

———. *God and You: Prayer as a Personal Relationship*. Mahwah, NJ: Paulist Press, 1987.

Barry, William A., and William J. Connolly. *The Practice of Spiritual Direction*. San Francisco: Harper and Row, 1982.

Blass, Virginia A. *Loaves and Fishes: From Faith Experience to Empowered Community*. Mahwah, NJ: Paulist Press, 1995.

Brackley, Dean, SJ. *The Call to Discernment in Troubled Times: New Perspectives on the Transformative Wisdom of Ignatius of Loyola*. New York: Crossroad, 2004.

Conroy, Maureen, RSM. *The Discerning Heart: Discovering a Personal God*. Chicago: Loyola Press, 1993.

———. *Experiencing God's Tremendous Love: Entering into Relational Prayer*. Mahwah, NJ: Paulist Press, 1988.

De Chardin, Pierre Teilhard, SJ. *Pierre Teilhard de Chardin: Modern Spiritual Masters Series*. Writings Selected with an Introduction by Ursula King. Maryknoll, NY: Orbis Books, 1999.

———. *The Divine Milieu*. New York: Harper and Row, 1965.

De Vinck, Christopher. *The Power of the Powerless: A Brother's Legacy of Love*. New York: Crossroad, 1988.

Eldredge, Becky. *The Inner Chapel: Embracing the Promises of God*. Chicago: Loyola Press, 2020.

English, John J., SJ. *Spiritual Freedom: From an Experience of the Ignatian Exercises to the Art of Spiritual Direction*. Guelph ON, Canada: Loyola House, 1983.

Francis, Pope. *Let Us Dream: The Path to a Better Future*. New York: Simon Schuster, 2020.

———. *Pope Francis' Little Book of Compassion: The Essential Teachings*. Edited by Andrea Kirk Assaf. Virginia: Hampton Roads Publishing, 2017.

Gallagher, Timothy M., OMV. *Discerning the Will of God: An Ignatian Guide to Christian Decision Making*. New York: Crossroad, 2009.

———. *Spiritual Consolation: An Ignatian Guide for the Greater Discernment of Spirits*. New York: Crossroad, 2007.

———. *The Examen Prayer: Ignatian Wisdom for Our Lives Today*. New York: Crossroad, 2006.

Ganss, George, SJ, ed. *The Spiritual Exercises of Saint Ignatius*. St. Louis: Institute of Jesuit Sources, 1992.

———. *Ignatius of Loyola: Spiritual Exercises and Selected Works.* Mahwah, NJ: Paulist Press, 1991.

Green, Thomas H., SJ. *Opening to God.* Notre Dame, IN: Ave Maria Press, 2006.

———. *Drinking from a Dry Well.* Notre Dame, IN: Ave Maria Press, 1991.

———. *Weeds among the Wheat: Discernment; Where Prayer and Action Meet.* Notre Dame, IN: Ave Maria Press, 1985.

Hansen, Michael, SJ. *The First Spiritual Exercises: Four Guided Retreats.* Notre Dame, IN: Ave Maria Press, 2013.

Haught, John F. *The New Cosmic Story: Inside Our Awakening Universe.* New York: Yale University Press, 2017.

Kiechle, Stefan. *The Art of Discernment: Making Good Decisions in Your World of Choices.* Notre Dame, IN: Ave Maria Press, 2005.

Kimmerer, Robin Wall. *Braiding Sweetgrass: Indigenous Wisdom, Scientific Knowledge, and the Teachings of Plants.* Minnesota: Milkweed Editions, 2013.

Martin, James, SJ. *Learning to Pray: A Guide for Everyone.* New York: HarperOne, 2021.

———. *The Jesuit Guide to (Almost) Everything: Spirituality for Real Life.* New York: HarperOne, 2010.

Nouwen, Henri. *Jesus: A Gospel.* New York: Orbis Books, 2001.

Nouwen, Henri J. M., Donald P. McNeill, and Douglas A. Morrison. *Compassion: A Reflection on the Christian Life.* New York: Doubleday, 1966.

Puhl, Louis J., SJ, ed. *The Spiritual Exercises of St. Ignatius.* Chicago: Loyola Press, 1951.

Ruffing, Janet K., RSM. *Spiritual Direction: Beyond the Beginnings.* Mahwah, NJ: Paulist Press, 2000.

Rupp, Joyce. *Boundless Compassion: Creating a Way of Life.* Notre Dame, IN: Sorin Books, 2018.

———. *Your Sorrow is My Sorrow.* New York: Crossroad, 1999.

———. *Little Pieces of Light…: Darkness and Personal Growth.* Mahwah, NJ: Paulist Press, 1994.

Ryan, Robin, CP. *Gazing on the Face of Christ: A Christ-Centered Spirituality.* Mahwah, NJ: Paulist Press, 2020.

Savary, Louis M. *Teilhard de Chardin: The Divine Milieu Explained; A Spirituality for the 21st Century.* Mahwah, NJ: Paulist Press, 2007.

Silf, Margaret. *At Sea with God: A Spiritual Guidebook to the Heart and Soul.* Notre Dame, IN: Sorin Books, 2008.

———. *Inner Compass: An Invitation to Ignatian Spirituality.* Chicago: Loyola Press, 1999.

Skehan, James W., SJ. *Praying with Teilhard de Chardin: Companions for the Journey.* Winona, MN: St. Mary's Press, 2000.

———. *Place Me with Your Son: Ignatian Spirituality in Everyday Life.* Washington, DC: Georgetown University Press, 1991.

Sparough, J. Michael, SJ, Jim Manney, and Tim Hipskind, SJ. *What's Your Decision?: How to Make Choices with Confidence and Clarity; An Ignatian Approach to Decision-Making.* Chicago: Loyola Press, 2010.

Swimme, Brian, and Thomas Berry. *The Universe Story: From the Primordial Flaring Forth to the Ecozoic Era; A Celebration of the Unfolding of the Cosmos.* San Francisco: Harper San Francisco, 1992.

Tetlow, Joseph A., SJ. *Choosing Christ in the World: Directing the Spiritual Exercises of St. Ignatius of Loyola according to Annotations Eighteen and Nineteen; A Handbook.* St. Louis: The Institute of Jesuit Sources, 1989.

Wicks, Robert J. *Night Call: Embracing Compassion and Hope in a Troubled World.* Oxford, England: Oxford University Press, 2018.

———. *No Problem: Turning the Next Corner in Your Spiritual Life.* Notre Dame, IN: Sorin Books, 2014.

Wright, N. T. *Surprised by Hope: Rethinking Heaven, the Resurrection, and the Mission of the Church.* San Francisco: HarperCollins, 2008.

ARTICLES

Barry, William A., SJ. "Friends with God." *America Magazine* 195, no. 9 (October 2, 2006): 25–27.

———. "How Do I Know It's God?" *America Magazine* 186, no. 17 (May 20, 2002): 12–15.

Skehan, James W., SJ. "Exploring Teilhard's 'New Mysticism': 'Building the Cosmos,'" *Journal for the Study of Religion, Nature, and Culture* (previously named *Ecotheology*) 10, no. 1 (April 10, 2005): 11–34.

AUDIOBOOKS

Available on CD/DVD or as an audio download at www .learn25.com (formerly Now You Know Media).

Blass, Virginia, and Harry Cain, SJ. *Is That You, God? Ignatian Discernment for Our Day.* Rockville, MD: LEARN25, 2012.

———. *Putting Out into the Deep: An Ignatian Retreat.* Rockville, MD: LEARN25, 2012.

McDermott, Brian, SJ. *The Theology of Grace.* Rockville, MD: LEARN25, 2011.

———. *The Spiritual Exercises of St. Ignatius of Loyola.* Rockville, MD: LEARN25, 2008.

Ryan, Robin, CP. *God and the Mystery of Human Suffering* (12-Part Series). Rockville, MD: LEARN25, 2011.

Tetlow, Joseph A., SJ. *Discerning God's Will the Jesuit Way.* Rockville, MD: LEARN25, 2009.

RECOMMENDED RETREAT CENTERS

St. Joseph's Retreat House, Milton, MA (www.omvusa.org)

Campion Center, Weston, MA (www.campioncenter.org)

Gonzaga/Eastern Point Retreat House, Gloucester, MA (www
.easternpoint.org)

Miramar Retreat Center, Duxbury, MA (www.miramarretreat
.org)

Marie Joseph Spiritual Center, Biddeford, ME (www.mariejoseph
spiritual.org)

Cormaria Retreat Center, Sag Harbor, NY (www.cormaria.org)

Actively dedicated and committed to
the protection and care of our Earth-home:

Drumalis (a retreat and conference center), Larne, Northern
Ireland (www.drumalis.co.uk)

Genesis Spiritual Life & Conference Center, Westfield, MA
(www.genesisspiritualcenter.org)

Our Lady of Calvary Retreat Center, Farmington, CT (www
.ourladyofcalvary.net)

Notre Dame Spirituality Center, Ipswich, MA (www.ndspirit
ualitycenter.org)

Thomas Berry Center, A Passionist Retreat Center in Jamaica,
New York (www.thepassionists.org)

ECOLOGY AND OUR EARTH-HOME

Thomas Berry Foundation makes available a video and book
about the contribution and impact of Thomas Berry's dedication and work for the care and the protection of our earth-
home (www.thomasberry.org).

Forum on Religion and Ecology provides a great variety of information about the interface of world religions with ecological connections (fore.yale.edu).

Journey of the Universe tells an epic story in video about the emergence of the universe and the community of life presented with a new vision of our earth's future, as authored by Brian Swimme and Mary Ellen Tucker (www.journeyoftheuniverse .org).

Sisters of the Earth, Green Mountain Monastery and the Thomas Berry, CP, Sanctuary (Greensboro, VT) is the burial place of Thomas Berry, CP, who cofounded this Community of Sisters and laity dedicated to the mission of the care of Earth's healing and protection (www .greenmountainmonastery.org).

Center for Ecozoic Studies offers a vision of an ecozoic society, meaning Earth and humans living in a mutually enhancing relationship, and contributes to its realization through research, education, and the arts (www.ecozoicstudies.org).

St. Gabriel's Catholic Church, Toronto, Canada, is a wonderful example of a church that is ecologically designed for worship, in harmony with Earth, and inspired by the teachings of Thomas Berry, CP. It contains the "Stations of the Cosmos" and is the first church in Canada certified by the Leadership in Energy and Environmental Design (www.stgabrielsparish .ca).

The Deeptime Network is a global network of teachers, scientists, artists, scholars, religious, and activists from around the world who are engaging in the study of the "Universe Story" and are actively sharing this knowledge with others to help make best choices for our ourselves and the future of our planet (www.dtnetwork.org).

ABOUT THE AUTHOR

Virginia A. Blass, DMin, MA, MEd, is an experienced and certified spiritual director, preacher, retreat master, and author. Her ministry includes spiritual direction, guided retreats, preached parish missions and programs, and consultation. She was also a learning disabilities specialist and special education teacher. During the past twenty years, Virginia engaged in caregiving and accompaniment for her parents and her sister, Joanie, who was born with cerebral palsy and was unable to walk or talk.

Virginia has engaged in ministry in collaboration with both the Passionists of the St. Paul of the Cross Province and the Jesuits of the Tri-Province for many years. She has also developed several resources in areas of parish social outreach, retreats, and Ignatian Spirituality: *Loaves and Fishes: From Faith Experience to Empowered Community* (Paulist Press, 1995); *Is that You God? Ignatian Discernment for Our Day* (audiobook with Harry Cain, SJ; Learn25, 2012); and *Putting Out into the Deep: An Ignatian Retreat* audiobook with Harry Cain, SJ; Learn25, 2012).

She is presently a member of the Passionist Preacher's Mission Team and has offered parish missions with several Passionists over the years, and with Fr. Harry Cain, SJ. Virginia was delighted to have preached a parish mission in Florida with her uncle, Fr. Vincent Youngberg, CP. She resides in New Hampshire.